OUR
FATHER

With gratitude
to my recusant Catholic ancestors of Lancashire
and my parents, Edmund and Bernadette

OUR FATHER

A Biblical Meditation

on the Lord's Prayer

Sr Claire Waddelove osb

Gracewing

First published in England in 2020
by
Gracewing
2 Southern Avenue
Leominster
Herefordshire HR6 0QF
United Kingdom
www.gracewing.co.uk

ISBN 978 085244 967 7

Typeset by Gracewing

Cover design by Bernardita Peña Hurtado

Front cover: detail from The Last Judgement, Convent of San Marco,
Florence, by Blessed Giovanni of Fiesole, surnamed 'the
Angelic'.

Frontispiece to Chapter 1: Calligraphy and illumination by the Benedictine
nuns of St Cecilia's Abbey, Ryde.

Contents

Abbreviations

NOTE

All Biblical quotations are taken from the Revised Standard Version (Catholic Edition CTS) unless otherwise stated. This Bible gives the Hebrew numbering of the Psalms first, with that of the Greek Septuagint in brackets afterwards. The Douay Rheims Bible, when quoted, gives only the Greek numbering.

Acknowledgements

This book would not have been completed without the generous help of others. I would like to express my profound thanks to Rev. Mother Abbess Ninian Eaglesham for her blessing and support for this project; Dom Luke Bell OSB of Quarr Abbey for his encouragement and advice; Sr Rachel Appleby, Sr Constance Neame, Sr Anne Eason and my sister-in-law Valerie, for their labours in transforming my hand-written manuscript into a computerised document; and Rev. Dr Paul Haffner of Gracewing for his editorial assistance.

Foreword

I am glad Sr Claire has written this book, and glad of its publication. St Benedict warned the followers of his Rule against secret hoarding of material things. He wants them to accumulate another kind of treasure: the wisdom found in Scripture, the writings of the Fathers of the Church, the prayers of the Liturgy, the teaching of the Church, the testimonies of the wise and holy.

Sr Claire has been feeding on these rich pastures for many years and now is ungrudgingly sharing what she has found. This book is the mature fruit of a steady course of reading, prayer and reflection. With clarity and economy, it serves us good fare and the new wine of the Gospel. Like the Seer of the book of Revelation, Sr Claire has heeded the command, "Write what you see." We can be grateful for this.

In his Rule, St. Benedict also requires that his monks hear the Lord's Prayer twice a day, remembering their duty to forgive each other and come before the Father in peace.

One evening, preparing for bed, the twentieth-century Scottish poet Edwin Muir found himself, after years of prayerlessness, suddenly reciting the Lord's Prayer, or rather feeling it well up inside him. Of all Jesus' words, the Our Father—along with the Beatitudes, and the parables of the Prodigal Son and the Good Samaritan—has travelled the furthest into humanity. Sr Claire, by choosing it as her subject, stands in a long tradition. To use an image of the Fathers, she shows how its limpid words are deep enough for elephants to swim in and simple enough for little lambs not to drown in. Her *lectio* has become *oratio*, and so the Word returns to the One who spoke it and new connections between the Scriptures and life come to light.

This is not a book to rush through. Its wine is for savouring, chapter by chapter, its bread for thoughtful digestion. Put simply, this is good, wholesome stuff. May it find many readers.

✠ Hugh Gilbert OSB, Bishop of Aberdeen

Author's Preface

This started as a small, private study, but it grew like the mustard seed. The Biblical texts selected are, of course, only a sample; many others could have been included. No claim is made for this book to be a scholarly thesis or exegesis; it is simply the fruit of personal reading and participation in the Church's liturgy at Mass and the Divine Office in a contemplative, monastic community. It is offered to a general readership with the hope of encouraging that immersion in the sacred Scriptures and meditative prayer which brings closeness to God in a unified Christian life.

I pray that the seeds of the word thus scattered may bring forth the harvest desired by the Father. Please pray for me too, mindful as I am of the words of St John Henry Newman in his sermon *Self-denial the Test of Religious Earnestness*, "It is easy to make professions, easy to say fine things in speech or in writing ... Let not your words run on; force every one of them into action" (PS I, 5).

Ut in omnibus glorificetur Deus

If there is anything wise in this human life which might encourage us to maintain a serene soul in the midst of the cares and tumults of the world, it is especially, I think, meditation on and knowledge of the Scriptures.

St Jerome, *Commentary on Ephesians*, Preface

Introduction

O God, who gave the Priest Saint Jerome
a living and tender love for sacred Scripture,
grant that your people may be
ever more fruitfully nourished by your Word
and find it in the fount of life.

Collect, 30th September

Thy word is a lamp to my feet and a light to my path
(Psalm 119(118):105). The sacred Scriptures,
written under the inspiration of the Holy Spirit,
are at once God's revelation of himself, a guide to holiness
and a source of nourishment for the spiritual life. "For
what page or what word of the divinely authorised Old
and New Testament is not a most direct rule for human
life?" asks St Benedict in the final chapter of his Rule[1] (cf.
2 Timothy 3:16–17). Pope Benedict XVI echoes this in the
conclusion of *Verbum Domini,* emphasising also the role
of the Church, "We must never forget that all authentic
and living Christian spirituality is based on the word of
God proclaimed, accepted, celebrated and meditated
upon in the Church."[2]

"In the sacred books the Father who is in heaven comes
lovingly to meet his children and talks with them."[3] We are
privileged to be recipients of this divine initiative. Silent
attentiveness will help us to enter more deeply into the
intimate relationship with God that he desires. Cardinal
Sarah describes *lectio divina* as,

---

1.   *The Rule of St Benedict,* 73.

2.   Pope Benedict XVI, *Verbum Domini,* 121.

3.   Vatican II, *Dei Verbum,* 21.

> a moment of silent listening, contemplation and profound recollection in the light of the Spirit ... the Word read in silence accompanies us, enlightens us and feeds us ... This Word is loved, revisited regularly, sought out, because it is the Presence of the One who loves us eternally. Through it, he who seeks my soul is there. He meets me, and I meet him. He reveals himself to me, and he reveals me to myself.[4]

In the parable of the sower (Luke 8:5–15), Our Lord speaks of the word of God as seed. The fruitfulness, or lack of it, depends upon the quality of the soil which receives it. The seed which falls on the path, rocky ground or among thorns produces nothing. "As for that in the good soil, they are those who hearing the word, hold it fast in an honest and good heart, and bring forth fruit with patience" (v.15). We are invited to be this good soil, and Cardinal Ratzinger explains how: "To be soil for the Word means that the soil must allow itself to be absorbed by the seed, to be assimilated by the seed, to surrender itself for the sake of transforming the seed into life."[5]

This is the way for the Church and each of her members to bear fruit. Mary, the Mother of God, is our model. Her womb was fruitful soil for the seed of the Incarnate Word of God sown by the Holy Spirit; her heart was equally fruitful soil as she "kept" and "pondered" everything there (cf. Luke 2:19; 2:51). Like her, "we must once more become waiting, inwardly recollected people who in the depth of prayer, longing, and faith give the Word room to grow."[6]

---

4.   Robert Cardinal Sarah, *The Power of Silence* (San Francisco: Ignatius Press, 2019), pp. 240–241.

5.   Joseph Cardinal Ratzinger and Hans Urs von Balthasar, *Mary—the Church at the Source* (San Francisco: Ignatius Press, 2005), p. 15.

6.   *Ibid.*, p. 17.

The Old and New Testaments form a unity, the old preparing the way for and fully explained by the New, the New hidden in the Old and bringing it to fulfilment. They both proclaim the mystery of Christ, "the mystery hidden for ages and generations but now made manifest" (Colossians 1:26). He himself said so, "You search the scriptures, because you think that in them you have eternal life; and it is they that bear witness to me ... If you believed Moses, you would believe me, for he wrote of me" (John 5:39, 46). And after his Resurrection, "beginning with Moses and all the prophets, he interpreted to them in all the scriptures the things concerning himself" (Luke 24:27).

The words Christ speaks are those he has received from his Father, and it is in the light of these words that the final judgment will be made. "He who rejects me and does not receive my sayings has a judge; the word that I have spoken will be his judge on the last day" (John 12:48). The book of Revelation presents a vivid pictorial image of this saying when it speaks of the Word of God, also called Faithful and True, seated on a white horse, with the armies of the saints following him: "From his mouth issues a sharp sword with which to smite the nations ... On his robe and on his thigh, he has a name inscribed, King of kings and Lord of lords" (19:15–16). It is the sword of the Spirit, the word of God[7] (cf. Ephesians 6:17), which, according to the letter to the Hebrews, is "living and active, sharper than any two-edged sword, piercing to the division of soul and spirit, of joints and marrow, and discerning the thoughts and intentions of the heart" (4:12).

The Our Father is itself, of course, a Scriptural text (Matthew 6:9–13), but perhaps we have become too

---

7.   Cf. Scott Hahn, *The Lamb's Supper* (London: Darton, Longman and Todd Ltd, 2003), p. 134.

familiar with it to appreciate its depth and all its resonances. The following chapters look at each line through
the lens of the whole of Scripture. The pure light, so to
speak, is refracted into many colours as the different
themes underlying the prayer emerge; their inter-weaving
produces the beautiful tapestry which is our faith. For
indeed, a great part of Christian doctrine is implied in the
Lord's Prayer, as well as direction for Christian living and
a piercing examination of conscience.

The texts are to be read slowly, with the eyes of the
heart and pondered there. It is an exercise in *lectio divina*,
that absorbing reading of Scripture which is already
prayer. As St Teresa of Avila pointed out, praying the Our
Father can become a means of experiencing pure contem-
plation and union with God.[8] Having the Scriptures in our
mind and heart as we pray can help bring this about.

In his commentary, Pope Benedict draws out some
further implications. Pointing out that in St Luke's version
the Our Father is placed in the context of Jesus' own praying, he continues:

> Jesus thereby involves us in his own prayer; he
> leads us into the interior dialogue of triune love;
> he draws our human hardships deep into God's
> heart, as it were. This also means, however, that
> the words of the Our Father are signposts to
> interior prayer, they provide a basic direction for
> our being, and they aim to configure us to the
> image of the Son. The meaning of the Our Father
> goes much further than the mere provision of a
> prayer text. It aims to form our being, to train us
> in the inner attitude of Jesus.[9]

8.   St Teresa of Avila, *The Way of Perfection*, 30.
9.   Pope Benedict XVI, *Jesus of Nazareth* (London, New York and
     Berlin: Bloomsbury, 2007), p. 132.

The prophecy in Isaiah below is primarily understood as referring to Christ, the Word which goes forth from the Father's mouth to earth in the Incarnation and returns in glory at the Ascension, having accomplished the Father's will. Yet it can be fulfilled in us too, as we respond to the Holy Spirit speaking to each of us individually through the sacred Scriptures. May we cherish this divine word ever more deeply, finding there the living and loving presence of God who calls us to himself.

> For as the rain and the snow come down from heaven,
> and return not thither but water the earth
> making it bring forth and sprout,
> giving seed to the sower and bread to the eater,
> so shall my word be that goes forth from my mouth;
> it shall not return to me empty,
> but it shall accomplish that which I purpose
> and prosper in the thing for which I sent it
>
> (Isaiah 55:10–11).

OUR FATHER
WHO ART IN
heaven

Hallowed be Thy Name—
Thy Kingdom come,
Thy will be done on earth
    as it is in heaven
Give us this day our daily bread
And forgive us our trespasses
As we forgive those who
    trespass against us;
And lead us not into temptation,
But deliver us from evil.

                Amen.

I

Our Father
who art in Heaven

*Almighty ever-living God, whom, taught by the
Holy Spirit,
we dare to call by the name of Father,
bring, we pray, to perfection in our hearts
the spirit of adoption as your sons and daughters,
that we may merit to enter into the inheritance
which you have promised.*

Collect, 19th Sunday of the Year

It is the Incarnate, divine Son who fully reveals God the Father; he is his perfect image, the Word, the Wisdom of God made flesh. He shows us, through his life and teaching, what the Father is like. In Christ, the invisible God could be seen and touched.

Already in the Old Testament, God was recognized as the Father of his people, but he was never invoked as such in prayer;[1] it would have been considered disrespectful. Jesus was the first one to do so. It was his habitual way of praying, of which we are given glimpses, such as, "I thank thee, Father, Lord of heaven and earth, that thou hast hidden these things from the wise and understanding and

---

1. Cf. St John Chrysostom, *Homilies on the Epistle to the Romans*, 4,3; Joachim Jeremias, *"Abba": The Prayers of Jesus*. Quoted by Pope Benedict XVI in *Jesus of Nazareth Part Two* (San Francisco, Ignatius Press, 2011), pp. 161–2.

revealed them to babes" (Matthew 11:25). It is used with particular frequency in Chapter 17 of St John's gospel, Jesus' high-priestly prayer.

As the second person of the Blessed Trinity, he is Son of the Father by nature, the eternal Son in a unique way which we, mere creatures, can never attain. "Thou art my son, this day have I begotten thee" (Psalm 2:7); "from the womb before the day star I begot thee" (Psalm 109:3).[2] He always refers to his Father as "my", "your" or "the" Father, and markedly does not include himself in the "our": "I am ascending to my Father and your Father, to my God and your God" (John 20:17).

Yet, what he is by nature, we can share in through the sanctifying grace of Baptism. We are given new birth in God, receiving supernatural life, becoming members of Christ's Body, adopted children of the heavenly Father, partakers in the divine nature. We have Christ's life, his Spirit, within us. As Pope St John Paul II assures us: "Rising from the waters of the baptismal font, every Christian hears again the voice that was once heard on the banks of the Jordan River: 'You are my beloved Son; with you I am well pleased' (Luke 3:22)."[3]

In teaching us to pray, therefore, Our Lord gives us the great privilege of addressing God with filial love and confidence:

> In this one word, Father, we voice our faith, our child-like trust, our surrender, our love, our contrition, our petition, our will to live for Him, to yield ourselves in everything to His holy will for us. Our Christian prayer, therefore, is not just the expression of purely

---

2. Vulgate, as translated in the Douay Rheims Bible. Both these texts are used in the Gregorian chants of Midnight Mass at Christmas.
3. Pope St John Paul II, *Christi fideles laici*, 11, 3.

natural man's relation with God who created him.
We come to Him in our prayers rather as children to
their heavenly Father, to praise, bless and love Him,
to petition Him for the help we require.[4]

The invocation of God as "our" Father emphasizes that we are not isolated individuals but members of one family. We all have God as our Father; each of us is precious to him and this has implications for the way we regard others, for the way we treat them. "This is the message which you have heard from the beginning, that we should love one another" (1 John 3:11). We are warned against rivalry and envy that can result in the enmity which led Cain to murder his brother, "because his own deeds were evil and his brother's righteous" (1 John 3:12). And as Our Lord makes clear in the Sermon on the Mount, anger and insult are forms of murder (cf. Matthew 5:21–2). To this could be added the attitude of indifference which cares nothing for the welfare of others. Active charity is the touchstone of our love for God: "If we love one another, God abides in us and his love is perfected in us" (1 John 4:12).

"Who art in heaven" reminds us that we have not been created for this world only. Our true home and destiny is where God dwells in eternity—indeed, it is God himself and our eternal existence in his love.[5] Already, every baptized soul in a state of grace is God's dwelling place; we have heaven within us. The more we live in inner communion with our divine guest and the more we live from this still centre of our being, so much the more will we experience the peace and joy which he alone can give. Yet

---

4.   Dom Benedict Baur OSB, *In Silence with God* (Cork: The Mercier Press Ltd, 1955), p. 94.

5.   Cf. Joseph Cardinal Ratzinger, *Dogma and Preaching* (Chicago: Franciscan Herald Press, 1985), pp. 116–117, where this thought is developed more fully.

this is only a small foretaste of what is to come when we see God face to face.

St Paul would have us know "what is the hope to which he has called you, what are the riches of his glorious inheritance in the saints" (Ephesians 1:18), and St Bernard exhorts us:

> We must bestir ourselves, brethren: let us rise with Christ, let us seek the things which are above, let us savour the things which are above. Let us long for those who long for us, hasten to those who await us.[6]

We can look on our earthly life as an apprenticeship, a training-ground, a novitiate for the world to come. There, everything that is good and true will come to its fulfilment, while every tear shall be wiped away, every injustice made good and sorrow shall be no more. The thought of heaven is not only an encouragement and means of sustenance in the trials of this life, but also an antidote to the temptation of becoming too immersed in, too attached to, the comforts of this world, its trivialities, fleeting pleasures, addictions, honours and rewards. Let us not be diverted from our true goal; let us not despise the Promised Land (cf. Psalm 106(105):24).

> Do not lay up for yourselves treasures on earth, where moth and rust consume and where thieves break in and steal, but lay up for yourselves treasures in heaven ... For where your treasure is, there will your heart be also (Matthew 6:19–21).

We have been created and redeemed to enjoy the vision of God in glory for ever. Let us not settle for anything less, let us not sell our birthright for a mess of pottage, let us hasten to do now what will profit us for ever.[7]

6.   St Bernard, *Sermon 5 for the Feast of all Saints*, 6.
7.   Cf. *The Rule of St Benedict*, Prologue.

Subheadings of the Biblical meditation which follows

- God's fatherhood of his people was already acknowledged in the Old Testament.
- As a loving Father, he cares for his children ...
- ... and disciplines them.
- He laments their faithlessness, but longs to show mercy and draw them back.
- His tender love is likened to, and even surpasses, that of a mother.
- Jesus Christ, the eternal Son made man, is the definitive revelation of God the Father.
- The fullness of adoptive sonship comes through our incorporation into Christ, the beloved Son, through the Holy Spirit.
- God's fatherhood is pre-eminent.
- He exercises an ever-watchful care.
- As children of one Father, we are called to fraternal communion with each other.
- Love for the brethren is the proof of our love for God.
- Further exhortations to humility, love of enemies and good works, in order to be worthy children of God.
- Our Lord bids us to act not for human praise but to please our Father.
- In all our failures to behave as true sons and daughters, let us never lose trust in the mercy of God.
- Let us entrust ourselves into the safe hands of our Father, not only at the end of our life but every day, in preparation for that final surrender.
- Heaven, the dwelling place of God and Christ in glory, is our final destiny and true home.

God's fatherhood of his people was already acknowledged in the Old Testament

Deuteronomy 14:1

> You are sons of the Lord your God.

Isaiah 63:16

> Thou art our Father,
>   though Abraham does not know us
>   and Israel does not acknowledge us;
> thou, O Lord, art our Father,
>   our Redeemer from of old is thy name.

As a loving Father, he cares for his children ...

Deuteronomy 1:31

You have seen how the Lord your God bore you, as a man bears his son, in all the way that you went.

Hosea 11:1

> When Israel was a child, I loved him,
>   and out of Egypt I called my son.

... and disciplines them

Deuteronomy 8:5

Know then in your heart that, as a man disciplines his son, the Lord your God disciplines you.

Proverbs 3:12

> The Lord reproves him whom he loves,
>   as a father the son in whom he delights.

He laments their faithlessness, but longs to show mercy and draw them back

Deuteronomy 32:6, 18–20

> Do you thus requite the Lord,
>   you foolish and senseless people?
> Is not he your father, who created you,
>   who made you and established you? ...
> You were unmindful of the Rock that begot you,
>   and you forgot the God who gave you birth.
> The Lord saw it, and spurned them,
>   because of the provocation of his sons and
>   daughters.
> And he said, "I will hide my face from them,
>   I will see what their end will be,
> for they are a perverse generation,
>   children in whom is no faithfulness."

Jeremiah 3:19, 22

> I thought how I would set you among my sons,
> and gave you a pleasant land,
>   a heritage most beauteous of all the nations.
> And I thought you would call me, My Father,
>   and would not turn from following me ...
> Return O faithless sons,
>   I will heal your faithlessness.

Tobit 13:4–6

> He is our Lord and God,
>   he is our Father for ever.
> He will afflict us for our iniquities;
>   and again he will show mercy ...
> If you turn to him with all your heart and with all
> your soul,
>   to do what is true before him

then he will turn to you
and will not hide his face from you.

Jeremiah 31:3, 9

I have loved you with an everlasting love;
therefore I have continued my faithfulness to you.
... with consolations I will lead them back,
I will make them walk by brooks of water,
in a straight path in which they shall not stumble;
for I am a father to Israel,
and Ephraim is my first-born.

His tender love is likened to, and even surpasses, that of a mother

Isaiah 66:13

As one whom his mother comforts, so I will comfort you.

Isaiah 49:15–16

Can a woman forget her sucking child,
that she should have no compassion on the son of
her womb?
Even these may forget,
yet I will not forget you.
Behold, I have graven you on the palms of my hands.

Jesus Christ, the eternal Son made man, is the definitive revelation of God the Father

Hebrews 1:1

In many and various ways God spoke of old to our fathers
by the prophets; but in these last days he has spoken to us
by a Son.

Matthew 11:27

All things have been delivered to me by my Father; and no one knows the Son except the Father, and no one knows the Father except the Son and anyone to whom the Son chooses to reveal him.

John 14:9, 11

He who has seen me has seen the Father ... Believe me that I am in the Father and the Father in me.

The fullness of adoptive sonship comes through our incorporation into Christ, the beloved Son, through the Holy Spirit

Ephesians 1:5

He destined us in love to be his sons through Jesus Christ, according to the purpose of his will.

Romans 8:14–16

All who are led by the Spirit of God are sons of God. For you did not receive the spirit of slavery to fall back into fear, but you have received the spirit of sonship. When we cry, "Abba! Father!" it is the Spirit himself bearing witness with our spirit that we are children of God.

Galatians 3:26–27

In Christ Jesus you are all sons of God through faith, For as many of you as were baptized into Christ have put on Christ.

1 John 3:2

Beloved, we are God's children now; it does not yet appear what we shall be, but we know that when he appears we shall be like him, for we shall see him as he is.

God's fatherhood is pre-eminent

Matthew 23:9

Call no man your father on earth, for you have one Father, who is in heaven.

Ephesians 3:14

I bow my knees before the Father, from whom every family in heaven and on earth is named.

Ephesians 4:5–6

... one Lord, one faith, one baptism, one God and Father of us all, who is above all and through all and in all.

He exercises an ever-watchful care

Matthew 10:29–31

Are not two sparrows sold for a penny? And not one of them will fall to the ground without your Father's will. But even the hairs of your head are numbered. Fear not, therefore; you are of more value than many sparrows.

As children of one Father, we are called to fraternal communion with each other

Psalm133(132):1, 3

>Behold, how good and pleasant it is
>>when brothers dwell in unity! ...
>For there the Lord has commanded the blessing,
>>life for evermore.

1 Thessalonians 4:9–10

Concerning love of the brethren you have no need to have anyone write to you, for you yourselves have been taught by God to love one another; and indeed you do love all the brethren throughout Macedonia. But we exhort you, brethren, to do so more and more.

Love for the brethren is the proof of our love for God

1 John 3:10

By this it may be seen who are the children of God and who are the children of the devil; whoever does not do right is not of God, nor he who does not love his brother.

1 John 3:16–18

By this we know love, that he laid down his life for us; and we ought to lay down our lives for the brethren. But if any one has the world's goods and sees his brother in need, yet closes his heart against him, how does God's love abide in him? Little children, let us not love in word or speech but in deed and in truth.

1 John 4:20–21

If any one says, "I love God," and hates his brother, he is a liar; for he who does not love his brother whom he has seen, cannot love God whom he has not seen. And this commandment we have from him, that he who loves God should love his brother also.

Further exhortations to humility, love of enemies and good works, in order to be worthy children of God

Matthew 18:3–4

Truly I say to you, unless you turn and become like children, you will never enter the kingdom of heaven. Whoever humbles himself like this child, he is the greatest in the kingdom of heaven.

Matthew 5:44–46, 48

Love your enemies and pray for those who persecute you, so that you may be sons of your Father who is in heaven ... For if you love those who love you, what reward have you? ... You, therefore, must be perfect as your heavenly Father is perfect.

2 Thessalonians 2:16

May our Lord Jesus Christ himself, and God our Father, who loved us and gave us eternal comfort and good hope through grace, comfort your hearts and establish them in every good work and word.

1 Peter 1:17

If you invoke as Father him who judges each one impartially according to his deeds, conduct yourselves with fear throughout the time of your exile.

Our Lord bids us to act not for human praise but to please our Father

Matthew 6:1

Beware of practising your piety before men in order to be seen by them; for then you will have no reward from your Father who is in heaven.

Matthew 6:3

When you give alms, do not let your left hand know what your right hand is doing, so that your alms may be in secret; and your Father who sees in secret will reward you.

Matthew 6:6

When you pray, go into your room and shut the door and pray to your Father who is in secret; and your Father who sees in secret will reward you.

Matthew 6:17–18

When you fast, anoint your head and wash your face; that your fasting may not be seen by men but by your Father who is in secret; and your Father who sees in secret will reward you.

In all our failures to behave as true sons and daughters, let us never lose trust in the mercy of God

Luke 15:18–20, 24

"I will arise and go to my father, and I will say to him, 'Father I have sinned against heaven and before you; I am no longer worthy to be called your son; treat me as one of your hired servants.'" And he arose and came to his father. But while he was yet at a distance, his father saw him and had compassion, and ran and embraced him and kissed him. "... this my son was dead and is alive again; he was lost, and is found." And they began to make merry.

Let us entrust ourselves into the safe hands of our Father, not only at the end of our life but every day, in preparation for that final surrender

Luke 23:46

Father, into thy hands I commit my spirit.

Heaven, the dwelling place of God and Christ in glory, is our final destiny and true home

Hebrews 13:14

Here we have no lasting city, but we seek the city which is to come.

John 17:24–25

Father, I desire that they also, whom thou hast given me, may be with me where I am, to behold my glory which thou hast given me in thy love for me before the foundation of the world.

1 Peter 1:3–4

Blessed be the God and Father of our Lord Jesus Christ! By his great mercy we have been born anew to a living hope through the resurrection of Jesus Christ from the dead, and to an inheritance which is imperishable, undefiled and unfading, kept in heaven for you.

Revelation 21:1, 3–4

Then I saw a new heaven and a new earth ... and I heard a great voice from the throne saying, "Behold, the dwelling of God is with men. He will dwell with them, and they shall be his people, and God himself will be with them; he will wipe away every tear from their eyes, and death shall be no more, neither shall there be mourning nor crying nor pain anymore, for the former things have passed away."

II

Hallowed be Thy Name

Grant, O Lord,
that we may always revere and love your holy name,
for you never deprive of your guidance
those you set firm on the foundation of your love.

Collect, 12th Sunday of the Year

What is God's name? In answer to Moses' request, God revealed not a personal title — he is not one deity among others — but his fundamental identity: being itself. "I AM WHO I AM," or simply "I AM."[1] This sacred name YHWH, was treated with such respect by the chosen people that it was spoken only once a year by the high priest, and that in the inner sanctuary of the Temple on the Day of Atonement. At all other times it was replaced by "Lord".

Along with this revelation of absolute being came a hint, a foreshadowing of the future revelation of the Blessed Trinity, three persons in one God, in the oft-repeated formula: "I am the God of Abraham, the God of Isaac and the God of Jacob," (not simply "the God of Abraham, Isaac and Jacob,") and in the threefold "Holy, holy, holy" of Isaiah.[2]

---

1. Other possible renderings are, "I AM HE WHO IS", "I AM WHO AM" cf. *CCC* 206.

2. Another clue to the Trinity is found in Genesis 18, where the Lord appears to Abraham in the form of three men.

God alone is holy, the source of all holiness; his name is hallowed by praise and thanksgiving, but above all by the corresponding holiness of his people. He set apart his chosen people from other nations and consecrated them to himself: "You are a people holy to the Lord your God; the Lord your God has chosen you to be a people for his own possession" (Deuteronomy 7:6). The Temple in Jerusalem would be the place where his name would dwell, the place of his special presence, the place of sacrifice and worship.

A response was required of the people: a life lived in conformity with their privileged calling. Keeping the Ten Commandments was the condition for maintaining the covenantal relationship with God. In failing to do this, and especially by their worship of false gods, God's holy name was profaned. The Temple and God's presence there would not protect the chosen people in their infidelity. The Promised Land had been given by God to the Israelites as a place where the life of the covenant could be lived. When this was violated, exile was the inevitable consequence and their just desserts.[3] Yet God did not utterly forsake his people: he would vindicate his holiness in the sight of the other nations by restoring them, chastened and humbled, to their land.

All these seeds in the Old Testament came to full flowering and fruition in the New. Jesus Christ is the Name of God, the presence of God, made flesh. The name Jesus (Joshua), given by the angel at the Annunciation to both Mary and Joseph, means in Hebrew, "YHWH is salvation." In Pope Benedict's words:

> The mysterious name from Mount Horeb [is] here
> expanded into the statement: God saves. The, as it
> were, incomplete name from Sinai is finally

---

3.   Cf. Joseph Cardinal Ratzinger, *The Spirit of the Liturgy* (San Francisco: Ignatius Press, 2000), pp. 19–20.

spoken. The God who *is*, is the saving God, now present. The revelation of God's name, which began in the burning bush, comes to completion in Jesus.[4]

Our Lord himself used the divine name revealed to Moses, most clearly in the statement, "Before Abraham was, I am." We can also see a deeper significance in the descriptive titles Jesus gives himself in St John's Gospel: "I am the bread of life" (6:35); "I am the good shepherd" (10:11); "I am the way, the truth and the life" (14:6); "I am the true vine" (15:1). In some passages it is obscured by the English translation: for example, in St John's account of the storm at sea and Jesus walking on the water, his words to the disciples, translated as, "It is I; do not be afraid", could equally be rendered, "I am ..." (6:20).

He also does not hesitate to give himself the divine authority associated with God's name, an efficacious authority, as is attested by the signs and wonders worked in his name in the Acts of the Apostles.

In the high priestly prayer at the end of his mortal life, Christ Our Lord prays for his disciples and recapitulates his mission, an essential element of which was the manifestation of the Father's name—the whole reality of God, his being, his holiness, his love.

> Now Jesus can lay claim to a final and consummate act of holiness in "the hour", the lifting up, the gathering, the revelation of the glory of God and the glorification of the Son and the final revelation of his love for his own.[5]

---

4. Pope Benedict XVI, *Jesus of Nazareth. The Infancy Narratives* (London: Bloomsbury, 2012), p. 30.

5. Francis Moloney SDB, *Sacra Pagina. The Gospel of John* (Collegeville: The Liturgical Press, 1998), p. 469.

Pope Benedict explains:

> It is Jesus' acceptance of the horror of the Cross,
> his ignominious experience of being stripped of all
> dignity and suffering a shameful death, that be-
> comes the glorification of God's name. For in this
> way, God is manifested as he really is: the God
> who, in the unfathomable depth of his self-giving
> love, sets the true power of good against all the
> powers of evil.[6]

This one, supreme sacrifice, which replaced all the types
and shadows of the Old Testament, is re-presented daily on
the altar in the sacrifice of the Mass, offered "for the praise
and glory of his name."[7] It fulfils the prophecy of Malachi:

> From the rising of the sun to its setting my name
> is great among the nations, and in every place
> incense is offered to my name, and a pure offering;
> for my name is great among the nations, says the
> Lord of hosts (1:11).[8]

The Mass is the means, par excellence, by which we glorify
God, and indeed, by which he glorifies himself.[9] God's
name dwelling in the Temple at Jerusalem has become the
Eucharistic presence in the tabernacle of all our churches,
the body, blood, soul and divinity of Christ, who can never
be separated from the Father and the Holy Spirit.

---

6.   Pope Benedict, *Jesus of Nazareth Part Two*, pp. 156–7.

7.   From a prayer said at the Offertory of every Mass.

8.   St Irenæus, commenting on this verse, writes: "What is this name
     which is glorified among the nations if not that of our Lord, by
     whom the Father is glorified, and man is glorified as well? How-
     ever, because the name is proper to his own Son, and because it
     was by him, the Father, that the Word was made flesh, he calls
     this name his own." *Against Heresies* IV, 17, 6.

9.   Cf. Vatican II, *Sacrosanctum Concilium*, 7.

This dwelling of God with men on earth foreshadows the ultimate fulfilment of all scripture and liturgy in the heavenly Jerusalem. "He will dwell with them and they shall be his people and God himself will be with them" (Revelation 21:3). Those who have been faithful to their Lord will have his name inscribed on their foreheads, as they gaze on his face for all eternity.

So let us honour God's holy name, Father, Son and Holy Spirit, always and everywhere, with our lips and with our lives. May his name be sanctified in us and in the entire world. Let us allow him to sanctify us, to transform us with his love, so that we may bear witness to him, manifesting his holiness in the world, and making his name present.[10] Let us do everything for his glory, not our own, and reject the enticements of the false idols of this world which would take us by stealth from the love and worship and service of the one true God, our one true good. He has promised to be with us to the end of the world and he does not go back on his word.

---

10. Cf. Pope Francis, *General Audience* (27 February 2019).

Subheadings of the Biblical meditation which follows

• God reveals his name.

• The holiness of God.

• Exhortations to thanksgiving and praise of God's name.

• Appeals to God for help, for the glory of his name.

• The name of the Lord represents his presence; the temple was his particular dwelling place on earth.

• God's name is profaned by the idolatry and sins of his people; the temple will not protect them.

• The people of Israel suffer exile as a result of their infidelity, but God will show mercy to them for the sake of his own holy name.

• Jesus, the name given by the angel Gabriel, means, 'God Saves'.

• Our Lord uses of himself the sacred name of God revealed to Moses: I AM.

• The name of the Father and the Son are to be equally reverenced: honour for one is honour for the other.

• The glorification of God through Christ's Passion and death, in St. John's Gospel.

• Our Lord gives the power and authority for great signs and wonders to be worked in his name.

• These are accomplished even amidst persecution. The apostles rejoiced to suffer for the name of Jesus.

• Baptised in the holy name of the Blessed Trinity ...

• ... we are called to reflect that holiness in our lives, doing good deeds for the glory of God.

• The reward of those who are true to the word and name of God and the worship of him in heaven.

God reveals his name

Exodus 3:13–15

Then Moses said to God, "If I come to the people of Israel and say to them, 'The God of your fathers has sent me to you,' and they ask me, 'What is his name?' What shall I say to them?" God said to Moses, "I AM WHO I AM." And he said, "Say this to the people of Israel, 'I AM has sent me to you.' God also said to Moses, "Say this to the people of Israel, 'The Lord the God of your fathers, the God of Abraham, the God of Isaac, and the God of Jacob, has sent me to you': this is my name for ever, and thus I am to be remembered throughout all generations."

Isaiah 42:8

> I am the Lord, that is my name;
>> my glory I give to no other,
>> nor my praise to graven images.

Isaiah 43:10–11

> "You are my witnesses," says the Lord,
>> "and my servant whom I have chosen
> that you may know and believe me
>> and understand that I am He.
> Before me no god was formed,
>> nor shall there be any after me.
> I, I am the Lord,
>> and besides me there is no saviour."

The holiness of God

Leviticus 11:44–45

I am the Lord your God; consecrate yourselves therefore, and be holy, for I am holy ... For I am the Lord who

brought you up out of the land of Egypt, to be your God;
you shall therefore be holy, for I am holy.

Isaiah 6:3

> Holy, holy, holy is the Lord of hosts;
> > the whole earth is full of his glory.

1 Samuel 2:2

> There is none holy like the Lord,
> > there is none besides thee.

Exhortations to thanksgiving and praise of God's name

Tobit 12:6

Praise God and give thanks to him; exalt him and give
thanks to him in the presence of all the living for what he
has done for you. It is good to praise God and to exalt his
name. Do not be slow to give him thanks.

Psalm 113(112):1–3

> Praise the Lord!
> > Praise, O servants of the Lord,
> > praise the name of the Lord!
> Blessed be the name of the Lord
> > from this time forth and for evermore!
> From the rising of the sun to its setting
> > the name of the Lord is to be praised.

Isaiah 12:4

> You will say in that day:
> > "Give thanks to the Lord,
> > call upon his name;
> make known his deeds among the nations,
> > proclaim that his name is exalted."

Appeals to God for help, for the glory of his name

Psalm 74(73):10, 18, 21

How long, O God, is the foe to scoff?
  Is the enemy to revile thy name for ever? ...
Remember this, O Lord, how the enemy scoffs,
  and an impious people reviles thy name ...
Let not the downtrodden be put to shame;
  let the poor and needy praise thy name.

Psalm 79(78):9

Help us, O God of our salvation,
  for the glory of thy name;
deliver us, and forgive our sins,
  for thy name's sake.

The name of the Lord represents his presence; the temple was his particular dwelling place on earth

Deuteronomy 12:5

You shall seek the place which the Lord your God will choose out of all your tribes to put his name and make his habitation there; thither shall you go.

1 Kings 8:27–29
(Part of Solomon's prayer at the Dedication of the Temple)

But will God indeed dwell on the earth? Behold, heaven and the highest heaven cannot contain thee; how much less this house which I have built! Yet have regard to the prayer of thy servant and to his supplication, O Lord my God, hearkening to the cry and to the prayer which thy servant prays before thee this day; that thy eyes may be open night and day toward this house, the place of which thou hast said, "My name shall be there," that thou mayest hearken to the prayer which thy servant offers toward this place.

Psalm 76(75):1–2

> In Judah God is known,
>   his name is great in Israel.
> His abode has been established in Salem,
>   his dwelling place in Zion.

God's name is profaned by the idolatry and sins of his people; the temple will not protect them

Jeremiah 7:9–15

Will you steal, murder, commit adultery, swear falsely, burn incense to Baal, and go after other gods that you have not known, and then come and stand before me in this house, which is called by my name, and say, "We are delivered!"—only to go on doing all these abominations? Has this house, which is called by my name, become a den of robbers in your eyes? Behold, I myself have seen it, says the Lord. Go now to my place that was in Shiloh, where I made my name dwell at first, and see what I did to it for the wickedness of my people Israel. And now, because you have done all these things, says the Lord, and when I spoke to you persistently you did not listen, and when I called you, you did not answer, therefore I will do to the house which is called by my name, and in which you trust, and to the place which I gave to you and to your fathers, as I did to Shiloh. And I will cast you out of my sight.

The people of Israel suffer exile as a result of their infidelity, but God will show mercy to them for the sake of his own holy name

Ezekiel 20:39

As for you, O house of Israel, thus says the Lord, God: Go serve every one of you his idols, now and hereafter, if you will not listen to me; but my holy name you shall no more profane with your gifts and your idols.

Ezekiel 36:18–24

So I poured out my wrath upon them for the blood which they had shed in the land, for the idols with which they defiled it. I scattered them among the nations, and they were dispersed through the countries; in accordance with their conduct and their deeds I judged them. But when they came to the nations, wherever they came, they profaned my holy name, in that men said of them, "These are the people of the Lord, and yet they had to go out of his land." But I had concern for my holy name, which the house of Israel caused to be profaned among the nations to which they came. Therefore say to the house of Israel, Thus says the Lord God: It is not for your sake, O house of Israel, that I am about to act, but for the sake of my holy name, which you have profaned among the nations to which you came ... and the nations will know that I am the Lord, says the Lord God, when through you I vindicate my holiness before their eyes. For I will take you from the nations, and gather you from all the countries, and bring you into your own land.

Jesus, the name given by the angel Gabriel, means, "God Saves"

Luke 1:31

Behold, you will conceive in your womb and bear a son, and you shall call his name, Jesus.

Matthew 1:20–21

Joseph, son of David, do not fear to take Mary your wife, for that which is conceived in her is of the Holy Spirit; she will bear a son, and you shall call his name Jesus, for he will save his people from their sins.

Acts 2:21

Whoever calls on the name of the Lord shall be saved.

Our Lord uses of himself the sacred name of God revealed to Moses : I AM

John 8:58–59

Jesus said to them, "Truly, truly I say to you, before Abraham was, I am." So they took up stones to throw at him.

John 8:28

Jesus said, "When you have lifted up the Son of man, then you will know that I am he."

John 18:4–6

"Whom do you seek?" They answered him, "Jesus of Nazareth." Jesus said to them, "I am he" ... When he said to them, "I am he," they drew back and fell to the ground.

The name of the Father and the Son are to be equally reverenced: honour for one is honour for the other

Philippians 2:9–11

God has highly exalted him and bestowed on him the name which is above every name, that at the name of Jesus every knee should bow, in heaven and on earth and under the earth, and every tongue confess that Jesus Christ is Lord, to the glory of God the Father.

John 3:17–18

God sent the Son into the world, not to condemn the world, but that the world might be saved through him. He who believes in him is not condemned; he who does not believe is condemned already, because he has not believed in the name of the only Son of God.

John 5:22–23

The Father judges no one, but has given all judgment to the Son, that all may honour the Son, even as they honour the Father. He who does not honour the Son does not honour the Father who sent him.

The glorification of God through Christ's Passion and death, in St. John's Gospel

John 12:27–28

"Now is my soul troubled. And what shall I say? 'Father, save me from this hour'? No, for this purpose I have come to this hour. Father glorify thy name." Then a voice came from heaven, "I have glorified it, and I will glorify it again."

John 13:31–32

When he [Judas] had gone out, Jesus said, "Now is the Son of man glorified, and in him God is glorified; if God is glorified in him, God will also glorify him in himself, and glorify him at once.

John 17:1

Jesus ... lifted up his eyes to heaven and said, "Father, the hour has come; glorify thy Son that the Son may glorify thee."

Our Lord gives the power and authority for great signs and wonders to be worked in his name

John 14:13–14

Whatever you ask in my name, I will do it, that the Father may be glorified in the Son. If you ask anything in my name, I will do it.

Mark 16:17–18

These signs will accompany those who believe: in my name they will cast out demons; they will speak in new tongues; they will pick up serpents, and if they drink any deadly thing it will not hurt them; they will lay their hands on the sick, and they will recover.

These are accomplished even amidst persecution. The apostles rejoiced to suffer for the name of Jesus

Acts 3:6, 8

Peter said, "I have no silver and gold, but I give you what I have; in the name of Jesus Christ of Nazareth, walk" ... And leaping up he stood and walked and entered the temple with them, walking and leaping and praising God.

Acts 4:16–20

"What shall we do with these men? For that a notable sign has been performed through them is manifest to all the inhabitants of Jerusalem, and we cannot deny it. But in order that it may spread no further among the people, let us warn them to speak no more to any one in this name." So they called them and charged them not to speak or teach at all in the name of Jesus. But Peter and John answered them, "Whether it is right in the sight of God to listen to you rather than to God, you must judge; for we cannot but speak of what we have seen and heard."

Acts 5: 40–41

When they had called in the apostles, they beat them and charged them not to speak in the name of Jesus, and let them go. Then they left the presence of the council, rejoicing that they were counted worthy to suffer dishonour for the name.

Baptised in the holy name of the Blessed Trinity ...

Matthew 28:18–20

All authority in heaven and on earth has been given to me. Go therefore and make disciples of all nations, baptizing them in the name of the Father and of the Son and of the Holy Spirit, teaching them to observe all that I have commanded you; and lo, I am with you always, to the close of the age.

... we are called to reflect that holiness in our lives, doing good deeds for the glory of God

Philippians 1:9–11

It is my prayer that your love may abound more and more, with knowledge and all discernment, so that you may approve what is excellent, and may be pure and blameless for the day of Christ, filled with the fruits of righteousness which come through Jesus Christ, to the glory and praise of God.

1 Peter 1:14–16

As obedient children, do not be conformed to the passions of your former ignorance, but as he who called you is holy, be holy yourselves in all your conduct; since it is written, "You shall be holy, for I am holy."

Matthew 5:16

Let your light so shine before men, that they may see your good works and give glory to your Father who is in heaven.

The reward of those who are true to the word and name of God, and the worship of him in heaven

Revelation 3:12

He who conquers, I will make him a pillar in the temple of my God; never shall he go out of it, and I will write on him the name of my God, and the name of the city of my God, the new Jerusalem which comes down from my God out of heaven, and my own new name.

Revelation 15:4

Who shall not fear and glorify thy name, O Lord?
    For thou alone art holy.
All nations shall come and worship thee,
    for thy judgments have been revealed.

Revelation 22:3–5

The throne of God and of the Lamb shall be in it, and his servants shall worship him; they shall see his face, and his name shall be on their foreheads. And night shall be no more.

IIII

Thy Kingdom Come

... you anointed your Only Begotten Son,
our Lord Jesus Christ,
with the oil of gladness
as eternal Priest and King of all creation,
so that, by offering himself on the altar of the cross
as a spotless sacrifice to bring us peace,
he might accomplish
the mysteries of human redemption
and, making all created things subject to his rule,
he might present to the immensity of your majesty
an eternal and universal kingdom,
a kingdom of truth and life,
a kingdom of holiness and grace,
a kingdom of justice, love and peace ...

From the Preface of Christ, King of the Universe

The kingship of God is well rooted in the Old
Testament. He was recognised as King of Israel,
king of all creation and was invoked personally as
king even after the Israelites had asked for a human king
to rule them, to be like other nations. The hallmarks of this
divine kingship were truth, justice and righteousness. The
foundations were thus laid for the coming of Christ, son
of King David, the Holy One of God, Truth in person and
King of kings.

Moreover, there are prophecies which, while seemingly
speaking of an earthly king, for the most part go beyond the
merely human. They can only be fulfilled in Christ. Psalm

72(71), for example, both prays for and celebrates the king's concern for the poor, needy and oppressed. It prays for the universal extension of his kingdom in space and time, for all kings to "fall down before him, all nations serve him" (v.11), for prosperity and abundance. "May his name endure for ever, his fame continue as long as the sun! May men bless themselves by him, all nations call him blessed!" (v.17).[1]

When the angel Gabriel appeared to the Blessed Virgin Mary to announce the conception and birth of Jesus, he proclaimed that the child would be the heir to the Davidic throne and that his kingdom would last for ever. The time had come for the fulfilment of ancient prophecies. It was, however, a difficult truth for even the apostles to learn that Our Lord's kingship would not be a worldly one. At the very end, shortly before the Ascension, they were still asking, "Lord, will you at this time restore the kingdom to Israel?" (Acts 1:6). It has been a temptation to think in terms of secular power throughout the Church's history. The New Testament presents a different picture; it is a kingdom characterised by the Beatitudes. "Blessed are the poor in spirit ... Blessed are those who are persecuted for righteousness' sake, for theirs is the kingdom of heaven" (Matthew 5:3,10).

When Jesus began his public ministry, his first proclamation took up the call of his precursor, St John the Baptist, "Repent, for the kingdom of heaven is at hand." His power over sickness and evil spirits showed that the reign of God was being inaugurated. Indeed, Christ himself embodied that reign. In and through him, God was present and active in a new and definitive way, combatting evil and bringing his lordship of goodness and self-sacrificing love into the world.

1.   This psalm is used in the monastic Office of Vigils for such feasts as Christmas, the Epiphany and Christ the King. It is worth reading in full.

The many parables he preached show various aspects of the kingdom, and, as so often in the Scriptures, they have different layers of meaning. Christ himself is primarily the treasure hidden in the field and the pearl of great value. He is the one for whom it is worth giving all, worth sacrificing all. Yet in the differing circumstances of individual lives, the message varies. It could be a call to embrace the Catholic faith, where the fullness of truth and means of sanctification are to be found. It could be an invitation to follow a priestly or religious vocation. St Albert the Great also sees Christ in the merchant, "who searched and is searching still for fine pearls," these precious gems being human souls whom he "sought, found and acquired."[2] With these the walls and gates of the heavenly Jerusalem are adorned (cf. Revelation 21:18–21). For each one of them, for each one of us, he gave everything he had. We have been bought at a great price.

The grain of mustard seed has likewise been given multiple interpretations by the Fathers of the Church.[3] It is the Church, growing from a small beginning into a great tree, spread out all over the world. It is the seed of faith sown in the heart of believers, growing up unto eternal life. It is Christ himself, sown as a seed in the womb of the Blessed Virgin, crushed in his Passion, buried in the garden, rising to become a great tree. He becomes a seed again in the Eucharistic host, small and hidden, but the source of vigorous spiritual growth and fecundity.

The parables illustrate that the kingdom of God has an innate power to develop and increase, but this is not an automatic process. As with many aspects of the Christian

---

2.   St Albert the Great, *Sermons on Saints,* 24.

3.   Cf. *e.g.* St Ambrose, *Commentary on the Gospel of St Luke,* Book 7, 176–185; St John Chrysostom (attributed to), *Homily* 7; St Peter Chrysologus, *Sermon* 98.

life, three elements are at work: gift, receptivity and persevering response. The kingdom in the form of grace, faith and salvation is initially a gift, but not every soul will receive it. Among those who do receive it, not all will persevere. Hence the parables illustrate the co-existence of good and bad in the field and in the net. This is a warning against complacency. Simply being a member of the Church does not guarantee a good life or a good end. In troubled times on the other hand, when evil in the Church is painfully exposed, these parables give reassurance. Such evil is rightly shocking to us; it is no surprise to God. It has all been foreseen and foretold. It is, therefore, no reason to despair of the Church, or to abandon her. It must have contributed to Our Lord's sweat of blood in Gethsemane, but he still chose to entrust the Church to sinful men. Of the chosen twelve, one betrayed him, another denied him, and all ran away. It was not a promising start. For our part, let us do our bit for the kingdom by striving to cultivate virtues and cut down vices, without being discouraged by the fact that, in every one of us, some degree of human weakness and imperfection, some faults of character or temperament, will always remain, even alongside goodness and holiness.

A striking aspect of the parables is the reality of judgment; evil will not go unpunished. Moreover, there is a strong emphasis on the punishment of sins of omission. The whole of Chapter 25 of St Matthew's gospel is devoted to this. The first part (vv.1–13) is the story of the wise and foolish maidens. The fault of the foolish ones was that of not having a sufficient supply of oil for their lamps. Implied here is a lack of charity which fuels perseverance in good works, if Jesus' earlier admonition in this gospel is remembered: "Let your light so shine before men that they may see your good works and give glory to your Father who is in heaven" (5:16).

The second, the well-known parable of the talents (vv.14–30), teaches that graces given must be used and made profitable for ourselves and for others. Growth is an intrinsic requirement. It is a normal part of both natural and supernatural life. Without it, there is only deformity and decay. The account of the Last Judgment, which concludes the chapter, emphasises Christ's presence in each person. He so identifies himself with those in need that to serve them is to serve him. Those who failed to do good to others failed to do it to him, and the punishment is severe.

In contrast, the generosity of God is portrayed in the parable of the workers in the vineyard (Mt 20:1–16). Those hired for only one hour were given the same wage as those who had "borne the burden of the day and the scorching heat" (v.12*)*. It was not unjust; it was the wage which had been agreed. The kingdom of heaven is given to those like the "good" thief who grasp it at the last by a death-bed repentance, as well as to those who have served God all their lives. It is our joy to serve God and it has its own reward, even amidst trials and difficulties. Moreover, no one can presume on the grace of repentance at the eleventh hour, especially if it has been rejected earlier. If a call—to conversion, to a deeper love for God, a more whole-hearted service or a specific vocation—is not answered when it is given, it might be lost for ever.

"Thy kingdom come." By responding to the Lord's calls, by allowing him to become ever more sovereign in our hearts, minds and souls instead of our tyrannical ego and unruly passions, we foster the growth of his reign on earth. We pray too that all may be receptive to grace and divine inspirations, that all may seek what is good and true, that peace and forgiveness may take root in all hearts, that care for those in need, selfless service, integrity and adherence to God's law may characterize social and political life. The prayer for his kingdom to come, however, is ultimately one for the second coming of Christ in glory, when the victory over sin and evil will be definitive. "... the Church longs for the completed kingdom and, with all her strength, hopes and desires to be united in glory with her king."[4] The glorious vision in the book of Daniel will then be fulfilled, and the final invocation in the book of Revelation will be answered, "Come, Lord Jesus!" (22:20).

---

4. Vatican II, *Lumen Gentium*, 5.

Subheadings of the Biblical meditation which follows

- God was recognized as King over the whole of creation and over Israel.
- Justice and righteousness are the hallmarks of his kingship.
- God was invoked personally as King.
- Old Testament texts on kingship which are, or will be, fulfilled in Christ.
- The proclamation of the angel Gabriel concerning Jesus at the Annunciation to Mary.
- Jesus preaches the kingdom of God; he is that kingdom in person.
- Signs of the kingdom: healing and exorcisms.
- The essence of Christ's kingship is witness to the truth.
- We follow a crucified King.
- His work of redemption effects the forgiveness of sins and entrance into his kingdom.
- The kingdom of heaven has small beginnings, but a power of its own to grow and be influential.
- Growth is not automatic; receptivity to Christ's gift is necessary.
- Seeking God and his kingdom is to take first place in our lives. Jesus rebukes the hesitant and half-hearted.
- The kingdom of heaven is worth every sacrifice.
- Warnings and admonitions to upright behaviour for the sake of the kingdom.
- The kingdom on earth contains both good and bad. There will be judgment and separation at the end of time.
- Sins of omission will also be judged severely.

- The Transfiguration gives a preview of Christ in glory.
- Our Lord's prophecy of the end of the world and his second coming.
- The fulfilment of the kingship of Christ and the kingdom of God in heaven.

God was recognized as King over the whole of creation and over Israel

Isaiah 43:15

I am the Lord, your Holy One, the Creator of Israel, your King.

1 Chronicles 29:10–12

David said: "Blessed art thou, O Lord, the God of Israel our father, for ever and ever. Thine, O Lord, is the greatness, and the power, and the glory, and the victory, and the majesty; for all that is in the heavens and in the earth is thine; thine is the kingdom, O Lord, and thou art exalted as head above all. Both riches and honour come from thee, and thou rulest over all. In thy hand are power and might; and in thy hand it is to make great and to give strength to all."

Psalm 95(94):3–5

> The Lord is a great God,
>   and a great King above all gods.
> In his hand are the depths of the earth;
>   the heights of the mountains are his also.
> The sea is his, for he made it;
>   for his hands formed the dry land.

Justice and righteousness are the hallmarks of his kingship

Psalm 9:7–8

> The Lord sits enthroned for ever,
>   he has established his throne for judgment;
> and he judges the world with righteousness,
>   he judges the people with equity.

2 Maccabees 1:24–25

O Lord, Lord God, Creator of all things, who art awe-inspiring and strong and just and merciful, who alone art King and art kind, who alone art bountiful, who alone art just and almighty and eternal ...

God was invoked personally as King

Psalm 5:2

> Hearken to the sound of my cry,
>   my King and my God,
> for to thee do I pray.

Psalm 145(144):1, 13

> I will extol thee, my God and King,
>   and bless thy name for ever and ever ...
> Thy kingdom is an everlasting kingdom
>   and thy dominion endures throughout all generations.

Old Testament texts on kingship which are, or will be, fulfilled in Christ

1 Chronicles 17:11–14

I will raise up your offspring after you, one of your own sons, and I will establish his kingdom. He shall build a house for me, and I will establish his throne for ever. I will be his father, and he shall be my son; I will not take my steadfast love from him ... but I will confirm him in my house and in my kingdom for ever and his throne shall be established for ever.

Zechariah 9:9–10

> Rejoice greatly, O daughter of Zion!
>   Shout aloud, O daughter of Jerusalem!
> Lo your king comes to you;
>   triumphant and victorious is he,
> humble and riding on an ass,
>   on a colt the foal of an ass.

I will cut off the chariot from Ephraim
    and the war horse from Jerusalem;
and the battle bow shall be cut off,
    and he shall command peace to the nations;
his dominion shall be from sea to sea,
    and from the River to the ends of the earth.

Daniel 7:13–14

I saw in the night visions,
    and behold, with the clouds of heaven
there came one like a son of man,
    and he came to the Ancient of Days
and was presented before him.
    And to him was given dominion
and glory and kingdom,
    that all peoples, nations and languages
should serve him;
    his dominion is an everlasting dominion,
which shall not pass away,
    and his kingdom one that shall not be destroyed.

The proclamation of the angel Gabriel concerning Jesus at the Annunciation to Mary

Luke 1:32–33

He will be great, and will be called the Son of the Most High; and the Lord God will give to him the throne of his father David, and he will reign over the house of Jacob for ever; and of his kingdom there will be no end.

Jesus preaches the kingdom of God; he is that kingdom in person

Mark 1:14–15

After John was arrested, Jesus came into Galilee, preaching the gospel of God, and saying, "The time is fulfilled, and the kingdom of God is at hand; repent, and believe in the gospel."

Luke 17:20–21

Being asked by the Pharisees when the kingdom of God was coming, he answered them, "The kingdom of God is not coming with signs to be observed; nor will they say, 'Lo, here it is!' or 'There!' for behold, the kingdom of God is in the midst of you."

Signs of the kingdom: healing and exorcisms

Matthew 4:23 cf. 9:35

He went about all of Galilee, teaching in their synagogues and preaching the gospel of the kingdom and healing every disease and every infirmity among the people.

Matthew 12:28

If it is by the Spirit of God that I cast out demons, then the kingdom of God has come upon you.

The essence of Christ's kingship is witness to the truth

John 18:33, 36–37

"Are you the King of the Jews? ... My kingship is not of this world, if my kingship were of this world, my servants would fight, that I might not be handed over to the Jews; but my kingship is not from the world." Pilate said to him, "So you are a king?" Jesus answered, "You say that I am a king. For this I was born, and for this I have come into the world, to bear witness to the truth. Everyone who is of the truth hears my voice."

We follow a crucified King

Matthew 27:27–31

Then the soldiers of the governor took Jesus into the praetorium, and they gathered the whole battalion before him. And they stripped him and put a scarlet robe upon him, and plaiting a crown of thorns they put it on his head, and put a reed in his right hand. And kneeling before him they mocked him, saying, "Hail, King of the Jews!" And they spat upon him, and took the reed and struck him on the head. And when they had mocked him, they stripped him of the robe, and put his own clothes on him, and led him away to crucify him.

John 19:19–22

Pilate also wrote a title and put it on the cross; it read, "Jesus of Nazareth, the King of the Jews." Many of the Jews read this title, for the place where Jesus was crucified was near the city; and it was written in Hebrew, in Latin, and in Greek. The chief priests of the Jews then said to Pilate, "Do not write, 'The King of the Jews,' but, 'This man said, I am the King of the Jews.'" Pilate answered, "What I have written I have written."

His work of redemption effects the forgiveness of sins and entrance into his kingdom

Luke 23:42–43

"Jesus, remember me when you come in your kingly power." And he said to him, "Truly, I say to you, today you will be with me in Paradise."

Colossians 1:13–14

He has delivered us from the dominion of darkness and transferred us to the kingdom of his beloved Son, in whom we have redemption, the forgiveness of sins.

Revelation 1:5–6

To him who loves us and has freed us from our sins by his blood and made us a kingdom, priests to his God and Father, to him be glory and dominion for ever and ever. Amen.

The kingdom of heaven has small beginnings, but a power of its own to grow and be influential

Matthew 13:31–32

The kingdom of heaven is like a grain of mustard seed which a man took and sowed in his field; it is the smallest of all seeds, but when it has grown it is the greatest of shrubs and becomes a tree, so that the birds of the air come and make nests in its branches.

Mark 4:26–28

The kingdom of God is as if a man should scatter seed upon the ground, and should sleep and rise night and day, and the seed should sprout and grow, he knows not how. The earth produces of itself, first the blade, then the ear, then the full grain in the ear.

Growth is not automatic; receptivity to Christ's gift is necessary

Matthew 21:31–32

Truly, I say to you, the tax collectors and the harlots go into the kingdom of God before you. For John came to you in the way of righteousness, and you did not believe him, but the tax collectors and the harlots believed him; and even when you saw it, you did not afterward repent and believe him.

Matthew 22:1–3

The kingdom of heaven may be compared to a king who gave a marriage feast for his son, and sent his servants to call those who were invited to the marriage feast; but they would not come.

Seeking God and his kingdom is to take first place in our lives. Jesus rebukes the hesitant and half-hearted

Matthew 6:31–33

Do not be anxious, saying, "What shall we eat?" or "What shall we drink?" or "What shall we wear?" For the Gentiles seek all these things; and your heavenly Father knows that you need them all. But seek first his kingdom and his righteousness, and all these things shall be yours as well.

Luke 9:62

No one who puts his hand to the plough and looks back is fit for the kingdom of God.

The kingdom of heaven is worth every sacrifice

Matthew 13:44

The kingdom of heaven is like treasure hidden in a field, which a man found and covered up; then in his joy he goes and sells all that he has and buys that field.

Matthew 13:45

Again, the kingdom of heaven is like a merchant in search of fine pearls, who, on finding one pearl of great value, went and sold all that he had and bought it.

Warnings and admonitions to upright behaviour for the sake of the kingdom

Matthew 5:20

I tell you, unless your righteousness exceeds that of the scribes and Pharisees, you will never enter the kingdom of heaven.

1 Corinthians 6:9–10

Do you not know that the unrighteous will not inherit the kingdom of God? Do not be deceived; neither the immoral, nor idolaters, nor adulterers, nor homosexuals, nor thieves, nor the greedy, nor drunkards, nor revilers, nor robbers will inherit the kingdom of God.

Galatians 5:19–23

Now the words of the flesh are plain: immorality, impurity, licentiousness, idolatry, sorcery, enmity, strife, jealousy, anger, selfishness, dissension, party spirit, envy, drunkenness, carousing, and the like. I warn you, as I warned you before, that those who do such things shall not inherit the kingdom of God. But the fruit of the Spirit is love, joy, peace, patience, kindness, goodness, faithfulness, gentleness, self-control.

The kingdom on earth contains both good and bad. There will be judgment and separation at the end of time

Matthew 13: 47–50

Again, the kingdom of heaven is like a net which was thrown into the sea and gathered fish of every kind; when it was full, men drew it ashore and sat down and sorted the good into vessels but threw away the bad. So it will be at the close of the age. The angels will come out and separate the evil from the righteous, and throw them into the furnace of fire; there men will weep and gnash their teeth.

Matthew 25: 31–34

When the Son of man comes in his glory, and all the angels with him, then he will sit on his glorious throne. Before him will be gathered all the nations, and he will separate them one from another as a shepherd separates the sheep from the goats, and he will place the sheep at his right hand, but the goats at the left. Then the King will say to those at his right hand, "Come, O blessed of my Father, inherit the kingdom prepared for you from the foundation of the world."

Sins of omission will also be judged severely

Matthew 25:41–46

Then he will say to those at his left hand, "Depart from me, you cursed, into the eternal fire prepared for the devil and his angels; for I was hungry and you gave me no food, I was thirsty and you gave me no drink, I was a stranger and you did not welcome me, naked and you did not clothe me, sick and in prison and you did not visit me." Then they also will answer, "Lord, when did we see thee hungry or thirsty or a stranger or naked or sick or in prison, and did not minister to thee?" Then he will answer them, "Truly, I say to you, as you did it not to one of the least of these, you did it not to me." And they will go away into eternal punishment, but the righteous into eternal life.

The Transfiguration gives a preview of Christ in glory

Mark 9:1–3

"Truly I say to you, there are some standing here who will not taste death before they see the kingdom of God come

with power." And after six days Jesus took with him Peter
and James and John, and led them up a high mountain
apart by themselves; and he was transfigured before them,
and his garments became glistening, intensely white, as
no fuller on earth could bleach them.

Our Lord's prophecy of the end of the world and his second coming

Matthew 24:14

This gospel of the kingdom will be preached throughout
the whole world, as a testimony to all nations; and then
the end will come.

Mark 14:61–62

The high priest asked him, "Are you the Christ, the Son of
the Blessed?" And Jesus said, "I am; and you will see the
Son of man sitting at the right hand of Power, and coming
with the clouds of heaven."

The fulfilment of the kingship of Christ and the kingdom of God in heaven

1 Corinthians 15:22–26

For as in Adam all die, so also in Christ shall all be made
alive. But each in his own order: Christ the first fruits, then
at his coming those who belong to Christ. Then comes the
end, when he delivers the kingdom to God the Father after
destroying every rule and every authority and power. For
he must reign until he has put all his enemies under his
feet. The last enemy to be destroyed is death.

Revelation 11:15–17

Then the seventh angel blew his trumpet, and there were
loud voices in heaven, saying, "The kingdom of the world

has become the kingdom of our Lord and of his Christ, and he shall reign for ever and ever." And the twenty-four elders who sit on their thrones before God fell on their faces and worshipped God, saying, "We give thanks to thee, Lord God, Almighty, who art and who wast, that thou hast taken thy great power and begun to reign.

IV

Thy Will be Done on Earth as it is in Heaven

Bestow on us, we pray, O Lord,
a spirit of always pondering on what is right
and of hastening to carry it out,
and, since without you we cannot exist,
may we be enabled to live according to your will.

Collect, Thursday 1st Week of Lent

As God has no parts, his will is identical with his being, his goodness, his love, his mercy. There is nothing better for us, or for the world, than that his will be done. In heaven, it is so, and it would be heaven on earth if it were so here. That paradise was lost through the rebellion of our first parents against the commandment of God. Fallen mankind has been in rebellion ever since, ever trying to be his own god; hence the misery of the world.

God's will is expressed first and foremost in the Ten Commandments, which make explicit the law he has written on man's heart, the natural moral law. The history of the Old Testament tells the story of God's centuries-long effort to train the Israelites to walk according to his commandments, to be truly his people.

These commandments were ratified by the Incarnate Son of God. In all his teaching and particularly in the Sermon on the Mount (Matthew, 5–7), Jesus showed his divine authority as lawgiver: "You have heard that it was said to the men of old ... But I say to you ..." He took nothing away from the original commandments, but revealed their full scope and depth, their interior aspect and the extent of charity required. Indeed, it is the teaching of the New Testament that all the commandments are summed up in the twofold commandment to love God and neighbour. Reciprocally, the keeping of the commandments is the proof of our love.

Our Lord is the perfect example of obedience to the Father's will. From it he drew his life and being. It was his whole mission, the driving force of his activity. He praised the faith of the centurion, (cf. Matthew 8:5–10) because that gentile could see that Jesus derived his miraculous power from a higher authority: because he obeyed his Father, the forces of nature would obey him, just as the centurion obeyed his commander and could therefore expect obedience from the soldiers under him.[1] He was also obedient to the written word of God. The gospels are punctuated by such sayings as, "All this has taken place, that the scriptures of the prophets might be fulfilled" (Matthew 26:56). "It is from the Scriptures that he takes the 'must be' (*dei*) which governs his whole life."[2]

This obedience and his love, both for his Father and for mankind, took him to Calvary. "Greater love has no man than this, that a man lay down his life for his friends" (John 15:13). And as St Paul says, "God shows his love for us in that while we were yet sinners Christ died for us" (Romans 5:8).

The chalice of suffering which, in Gethsemane, he entreated his Father to remove from him, was not merely that of a cruel death, but the weight of all the sin in the world in the whole of human history. "For our sake he

---

1.   Cf. Raniero Cantalamessa, *Obedience* (Slough: St Paul Publications, 1989), pp. 63–64.

2.   *Ibid.*, p. 19.

made him to be sin who knew no sin" (2 Corinthians 5:21). Through the agonized prayer of Jesus, "nevertheless not my will, but thine, be done", his human will was drawn into harmony with his divine will, and that on behalf of us all. As Pope Benedict writes:

> In Jesus' natural human will, the sum total of human nature's resistance to God, is, as it were, present within Jesus himself. The obstinacy of us all, the whole of our opposition to God is present, and in his struggle, Jesus elevates our recalcitrant nature to become its real self.[3]

Through his sacrifice of obedience, through his filial abandonment to the Father's will, we have been redeemed. Furthermore, Christ has won for us the necessary grace and given us the example to follow when faced with moral crises in our own life. In the words of St Augustine:

> O Lord, our Mediator, God who transcends us, made man for our sake, I recognize your great mercy! For you are troubled in your will by reason of your immense love, so that you console and pre-serve from despair the many members of your body who are troubled because of their weakness ... Per-haps a moment of crisis may arise: we are faced with the option of either doing wrong or of undergoing suffering. The weak soul is troubled, but the invincible soul of the Lord was voluntarily troubled on her behalf; submit your will to that of God.[4]

Knowing our weakness, Mother Church gives us in the liturgy a prayer to help in times of need: "... even when our wills are defiant, constrain them mercifully to turn to

---

3. Pope Benedict, *Jesus of Nazareth Part Two* p. 161.
4. St Augustine, *Homilies on St John's Gospel*, 52:2–3.

you."[5] God respects our free will, but we can ask him to give us a push, so to speak, when we know that there is something we should do, something or someone that we should give up, but can't quite bring our self to do it.

How do we discern God's will for us in our life? Fundamentally, we are taught or given it by the Commandments, the Church's Magisterium,[6] legitimate Superiors, the ordinary duties of our state in life and by the daily circumstances and events which are outside our control. Beyond these, we seek it through prayer and the meditative reading of the Scriptures and other spiritual writings,[7] through regular sacramental confession and by cultivating a listening heart which genuinely abandons itself to God in filial confidence. If we have our own fixed plans and merely want God to rubber-stamp them, if we try in our prayers to bludgeon God into doing our will, then we are not open to what he wants to say to us. Silent attention to God's presence will enable us to hear the still small voice of the Holy Spirit. "Speak, Lord, for thy servant hears" (1 Samuel 3:9).

Endless distractions, noise, breathless busyness, an excess of superficial exchanges via the Internet, all impede God's communication. "To refuse silence filled with confident fear and adoration is to refuse God the freedom to take hold of us by his love and presence. Sacred silence allows man to place himself joyfully at God's disposal."[8]

5. Prayer over the Offerings, Saturday 4th Week of Lent.
6. The *Catechism* has a wealth of material for the formation of a good conscience, notably in Part Three, Life in Christ.
7. Guidance can be found in many spiritual classics such as the works of St John of the Cross and the *Spiritual Exercises* of St Ignatius Loyola. A small modern book can be commended: Jacques Philippe, *In the School of the Holy Spirit* (New York: Scepter Publishers, 2007).
8. Sarah, *The Power of Silence*, p. 121.

Furthermore, a measure of self-denial in our life is necessary to train us to be responsive to God's designs. For if we always indulge our whims and fancies, always pursue what seems best for ourselves rather than for others, we won't be able to answer his call, even if we hear it.

Response to what we do discern as God's will is all important. His purpose is our sanctification. To do with love the will of God, and to will with love what God does, is the essence of holiness. As we grow in docility to grace, more will be given us. If we harden our hearts and knowingly refuse the divine will, we will become lukewarm, perhaps fall away, lose our sense of divine guidance and become prey to temptation. St John Henry Newman exhorts us:

> Act up to your light, though in the midst of difficulties, and you will be carried on, you do not know how far. Abraham obeyed the call and journeyed, not knowing whither he went; so we, if we follow the voice of God, shall be brought on step by step into a new world … but when men refuse to profit by light already granted, their light is turned to darkness.[9]

If "Thy will be done" is at the heart of all our prayers, we are safe in the hands of our heavenly Father. "We know that in everything God works for good with those who love him" (Romans 8:28). "Everything" includes the ill will of others. In the book of Genesis, Joseph was sold into slavery by his brothers, but their misdeed became the means by which their lives and many others were saved in time of famine. "As for you, you meant evil against me; but God meant it for good, to bring it about that many people should be kept alive, as they are today" (Genesis 50:20).

---

9.   St John Henry Newman, PS. VIII, 13, "Truth hidden when not sought after", (London, Oxford & Cambridge: Rivingtons, 1868), pp. 195–196.

This episode prefigures the selling of Jesus into captivity and death. The letter to the Hebrews asserts that his prayers to be saved from death were heard. He did die, but was saved out of death, rising to a new, glorious, imperishable life, becoming the source of eternal salvation for the whole of mankind. His executioners meant evil against him, but God meant it for good. Baldwin of Ford expresses it beautifully:

> Those who shed Christ's blood did not think or act with the intention of taking away the sins of the world; but nevertheless, they were unconsciously serving the plan of salvation. The salvation of the world which ensued was not the result of their power, their will, or their action, but came from the power, will, intention, and action of God. For in that outpouring of blood it was not only the injustice of the persecutors which was at work, but also the love of the Saviour. But injustice accomplished a work of injustice; love accomplished a work of love. It was not injustice but love that wrought our salvation.[10]

So let us entrust ourselves to this Love which always wills our good and which can turn every misfortune and adversity to our benefit, for our life in eternity if not in time. Let us try to make our own Blessed Charles de Foucauld's prayer of abandonment:

> My Father, I put myself in your hands. I abandon myself to you. I entrust myself to you. Make of me what you will. Whatever you make of me, I thank you, I am ready for everything. I accept everything, I thank you for everything. Provided that your will be done in me, Lord, as in all your creatures, in all your children, in all those whom your heart loves, I desire nothing else. I put my soul in your hands,

---

10. Baldwin of Ford, *Treatise on the Sacrament of the Altar*, Part 2, 1.

I give it to you, Lord, with all the love in my heart,
because I love you, and because it is for me a need
of love to give myself, to put myself in your hands,
unreservedly. I put myself in your hands with
infinite trust, for you are my Father.[11]

---

11. Quoted in Jean-Jacques Antier, *Charles de Foucauld* (San
    Francisco: Ignatius Press, 1999), p. 312.

Subheadings of the Biblical meditation which follows

- The Ten Commandments are an expression of God's will.
- Exhortations to observe them for life and well-being.
- The Psalms and Wisdom literature praise the law of the Lord and encourage humble love.
- Personal desire and prayer to do the will of God.
- Trustful acceptance of God's will in grave circumstances.
- God proclaims his use of human instruments to achieve his purposes.
- Christ's example of perfect obedience to the will of his Father, even unto death.
- This loving obedience wrought our redemption.
- God's will for us: salvation and sanctification ...
- ... praise and thanksgiving.
- The necessity for us to do the will of God.
- Exhortations to seek God's will and live in accordance with it.
- The importance of obedience.
- The role of the Holy Spirit.
- Keeping the commandments is a proof of love and brings us closer to God.
- Love is the fulfilment of the commandments.

The Ten Commandments are an expression of God's will

Exodus 20:2–17

I am the Lord your God, who brought you out of the land of Egypt, out of the house of bondage.
You shall have no other gods before me ...
You shall not take the name of the Lord your God in vain ...
Remember the sabbath day, to keep it holy ...
Honour your father and your mother ...
You shall not kill.
You shall not commit adultery.
You shall not steal.
You shall not bear false witness against your neighbour.
You shall not covet your neighbour's house; you shall not covet your neighbour's wife ... or anything that is your neighbour's.

Exhortations to observe them for life and well-being

Deuteronomy 30:15–16

See, I have set before you this day life and good, death and evil. If you obey the commandments of the Lord your God which I command you this day, by loving the Lord your God, by walking in his ways, and by keeping his commandments and his statutes and his ordinances, then you shall live and multiply, and the Lord your God will bless you in the land which you are entering to take possession of it.

1 Kings 2:2–3

Be strong, and show yourself a man, and keep the charge of the Lord your God, walking in his ways and keeping his statutes, his commandments, his ordinances, and his testimonies, as it is written in the law of Moses, that you may prosper in all that you do and wherever you turn.

The Psalms and Wisdom literature praise the law of the Lord and encourage humble love

Psalm 19(18): 7–10

> The law of the Lord is perfect,
>> reviving the soul;
> the testimony of the Lord is sure,
>> making wise the simple;
> the precepts of the Lord are right,
>> rejoicing the heart;
> the commandment of the Lord is pure,
>> enlightening the eyes;
> the fear of the Lord is clean,
>> enduring for ever;
> the ordinances of the Lord are true,
>> and righteous altogether.
> More to be desired are they than gold,
>> even much fine gold;
> sweeter also than honey
>> and drippings of the honeycomb.

Proverbs 3:5–7

> Trust in the Lord with all your heart,
>> and do not rely on your own insight.
> In all your ways acknowledge him,
>> and he will make straight your paths.
> Be not wise in your own eyes;
>> fear the Lord and turn away from evil.

Personal desire and prayer to do the will of God

Psalm 40(39):6–8

> Sacrifice and offering thou dost not desire;
>> but thou hast given me an open ear.
> Burnt offering and sin offering

thou hast not required.
Then I said, "Lo, I come;
    in the roll of the book it is written of me;
I delight to do thy will, O my God;
    thy law is within my heart."

Psalm 143(142):8–10

Teach me the way I should go,
    for to thee I lift up my soul.
Deliver me, O Lord, from my enemies!
    I have fled to thee for refuge!
Teach me to do thy will,
    for thou art my God!
Let thy good spirit lead me
    on a level path!

Trustful acceptance of God's will in grave circumstances

1 Maccabees 3:58–60

And Judas said, "Gird yourselves and be valiant. Be ready early in the morning to fight with these Gentiles who have assembled against us to destroy us and our sanctuary. It is better for us to die in battle them to see the misfortunes of our nation and of the sanctuary. But as his will in heaven may be, so he will do."

Acts 21:10–14

While we were staying for some days, a prophet named Agabus came down from Judea. And coming to us he took Paul's girdle and bound his own feet and hands, and said, "Thus says the Holy Spirit, 'so shall the Jews at Jerusalem bind the man who owns this girdle and deliver him into the hands of the Gentiles.'" When we heard this, we and the people begged him not to go up to Jerusalem. Then Paul answered, "What are you doing, weeping and

breaking my heart? For I am ready not only to be im-
prisoned but even to die at Jerusalem for the name of the
Lord Jesus." And when he would not be persuaded, we
ceased and said, "The will of the Lord be done."

God proclaims his use of human instruments to achieve his purposes

Acts 13:22

He raised up David to be their king; of whom he testified
and said, "I have found in David the son of Jesse a man
after my own heart, who will do all my will."

Isaiah 44: 24, 28

I am the Lord who made all things ... who says of Cyrus,
"He is my shepherd, and he shall fulfil all my purpose."

Christ's example of perfect obedience to the will of his Father, even unto death

Luke 22:41–44

He withdrew from them about a stone's throw and knelt
down and prayed. "Father, if thou art willing, remove this
cup from me; nevertheless not my will, but thine, be done."
And there appeared to him an angel strengthening him.
And being in agony he prayed more earnestly; and his
sweat became like great drops of blood falling down upon
the ground.

Isaiah 50:5–6

> The Lord GOD has opened my ear,
>   and I was not rebellious,
>   I turned not backward.
> I gave my back to the smiters,
>   and my cheeks to those who pulled out the beard;

I hid not my face
    from shame and spitting.

Philippians 2:8

Being found in human form he humbled himself and became obedient unto death, even death on a cross.

This loving obedience wrought our redemption

Isaiah 53:10–11

Yet it was the will of the Lord to bruise him;
    he has put him to grief;
when he makes himself an offering for sin,
    he shall see his offspring, he shall prolong his days;
the will of the Lord shall prosper in his hand;
    he shall see the fruit of the travail of his soul and
    be satisfied
by his knowledge shall the righteous one, my servant,
    make many to be accounted righteous;
    and he shall bear their iniquities.

John 6:38–40

I have come down from heaven, not to do my own will, but the will of him who sent me; and this is the will of him who sent me, that I should lose nothing of all that he has given me, but raise it up on the last day. For this is the will of my Father, that every one who sees the Son and believes in him should have eternal life; and I will raise him up at the last day.

Romans 5:19

For as by one man's disobedience many were made sinners, so by one man's obedience many will be made righteous.

God's will for us: salvation and sanctification ...

Matthew 18:14

It is not the will of my Father who is in heaven that one of these little ones should perish.

1 Thessalonians 4:3–4

This is the will of God, your sanctification: that you abstain from immorality; that each one of you know how to control his body in holiness and honour.

... praise and thanksgiving

Ephesians 1:11–12

In him, according to the purpose of him who accomplishes all things according to the counsel of his will, we who first hoped in Christ have been destined and appointed to live for the praise of his glory.

1 Thessalonians 5:16–18

Rejoice always, pray constantly, give thanks in all circumstances; for this is the will of God in Christ Jesus for you.

The necessity for us to do the will of God

Matthew 7:21

Not every one who says to me, "Lord, Lord," shall enter the kingdom of heaven, but he who does the will of my Father who is in heaven.

Luke12:47–48

That servant who knew his master's will, but did not make ready or act according to his will, shall receive a severe beating. But he who did not know, and did what deserved a beating, shall receive a light beating.

Exhortations to seek God's will and live in accordance with it

Romans 12:2

Do not be conformed to this world but be transformed by the renewal of your mind, that you may prove what is the will of God, what is good and acceptable and perfect.

Hebrews 13:20–21

May the God of peace who brought again from the dead our Lord Jesus, the great shepherd of the sheep, by the blood of the eternal covenant, equip you with everything good that you may do his will, working in you that which is pleasing in his sight, through Jesus Christ; to whom be glory for ever and ever. Amen.

Hebrews 10:35–36

Do not throw away your confidence, which has a great reward. For you have need of endurance, so that you may do the will of God and receive what is promised.

The importance of obedience

1 Samuel 15:22–23

Samuel said,
  "Has the Lord as great delight in burnt offerings and
  sacrifices,
    as in obeying the voice of the Lord?
  Behold, to obey is better than sacrifice,
    and to hearken than the fat of rams.
  For rebellion is as the sin of divination,
    and stubbornness is as iniquity and idolatry."

Philippians 2:14–15

Do all things without grumbling or questioning, that you may be blameless and innocent, children of God without blemish in the midst of a crooked and perverse generation, among whom you shine as lights in the world.

James 1:22

Be doers of the word, and not hearers only, deceiving yourselves.

The role of the Holy Spirit

Wisdom 9:17–18

> Who has learned thy counsel, unless thou hast given wisdom
> and sent thy holy Spirit from on high?
> And thus the paths of those on earth were set right,
> and men were taught what pleases thee,
> and were saved by wisdom.

John 14:16–17

I will pray the Father, and he will give you another Counsellor, to be with you for ever, even the Spirit of truth.

Acts 13:2–3

While they were worshipping the Lord and fasting, the Holy Spirit said, "Set apart for me Barnabas and Saul for the work to which I have called them." Then after fasting and praying they laid their hands on them and sent them off.

Keeping the commandments is a proof of love and brings us closer to God

John 14:21

He who has my commandments and keeps them, he it is who loves me; and he who loves me will be loved by my Father, and I will love him and manifest myself to him.

John 15:14

You are my friends if you do what I command you.

Love is the fulfilment of the commandments

Matthew 22:36–40

"Teacher which is the great commandment in the law?" And he said to him, "You shall love the Lord your God with all your heart, and with all your soul, and with all your mind. This is the great and first commandment. And a second is like it, You shall love your neighbour as yourself. On these two commandments depend all the law and the prophets."

Romans 13:8–10

Owe no one anything, except to love one another; for he who loves his neighbour has fulfilled the law. The commandments, "You shall not commit adultery, You shall not kill, You shall not steal, You shall not covert" and any other commandment, are summed up in this sentence, "You shall love your neighbour as yourself." Love does no wrong to a neighbour; therefore love is the fulfilling of the law.

John 13:34

A new commandment I give to you, that you love one another; even as I have loved you, that you also love one another.

V

Give us This Day our Daily Bread

Renewed now with heavenly bread,
by which faith is nourished, hope increased,
and charity strengthened,
we pray, O Lord, that we may learn to hunger for
Christ,
the true and living Bread,
and strive to live by every word
which proceeds from your mouth.

Prayer after Communion, 1ˢᵗ Sunday of Lent

As the Scriptures relate, God, in his goodness, has provided amply for all our physical needs in his creation. Those of us who are fortunate enough not to be living in abject poverty might be tempted to take our daily bread for granted. In the prayer he gave us, Our Lord teaches us to pray that all may benefit from the fruits of the earth. The practice of saying grace before and after a meal reminds us that it is through God's bounty that we are fed, and that gratitude is due to him.

As early as the fourth chapter of Genesis, we are given the example of Abel who made an offering to the Lord of "the firstlings of his flock and of their fat portions" (v.4). The best was offered to God in thanksgiving. Two of the annual festivals established in the book of Exodus related to the harvest:

> You shall keep the feast of harvest, of the first fruits
> of your labour, of what you sow in the field. You
> shall keep the feast of ingathering at the end of the
> year, when you gather in from the field the fruit of
> your labours (23:16).

These offerings acknowledged mankind's utter dependence on God.

His generosity to us encourages us to be equally generous to those in need. We are stewards of God's blessings which are intended to be distributed and shared among all. An attitude of contentment with what is sufficient, rather than greed for what is luxurious or merely superfluous, will enable us to practise almsgiving. The parable of Dives and Lazarus, and the sorry end of the rich man who refused charity to the poor one, is a warning that we will be held accountable. Our charity or lack of it will determine our eternal destiny.

In addition to the provisions of the natural order, it is within God's power and will to provide food miraculously. Numerous examples of this are recounted in the Scriptures, the most charming surely being that of the prophet Habakkuk, grasped by the hair of his head by an angel, and transported to Babylon to give his dinner to Daniel in the lion's den! (cf. Daniel 14:33–39). The Lord often likes to make use of human contributions in these miracles; he takes the little we have and multiplies it. In 1 Kings 17:8–16, a widow was asked to take the little food she had left for herself and her son, and give it to the prophet Elijah, with the promise that there would be enough. She obeyed in faith and was rewarded with a supply which lasted until the end of the famine.

Such incidents have been repeated in the lives of some of the saints down the ages and in our own times too. Benedict Rogers writes of a religious sister in East Timor,

"Miraculous interventions were commonplace in Mana Lou's work." In 1999, she, and the Institute she had founded, for numerous weeks fed 15,000 people who had fled into the hills from violence in the capital. They had only one barrel of rice. Each morning she prayed and the rice did not run out until aid arrived.[1]

This exemplifies to a heroic degree the trust taught by Jesus, that we be not anxious about the material needs of the morrow, but seek first his kingdom. "Give us this day ..." It was a marked feature of the gift of manna to the Israelites in the desert that they could only gather enough for one day. When they tried to hoard it, it went bad. Psalm 95(94), which is sung every morning at Vigils, exhorts us, "O that today you would hearken to his voice! Harden not your hearts" (vv.7–8). The letter to the Hebrews takes this up, "Exhort one another every day, as long as it is called 'today'" (3:13). We are bidden to live one day at a time in the present, in the presence of God, attentive to him.

The Israelites were also taught that, "man does not live by bread alone". He has spiritual needs, a hunger for God, for grace, goodness, beauty and truth. Our Lord includes among the Beatitudes, "those who hunger and thirst for righteousness, for they shall be satisfied" (Matthew 5:6). Commenting on Mary of Bethany who sat at Our Lord's feet in Chapter 10 of St Luke's Gospel, St Augustine quotes this verse, and continues:

> It was the truth which delighted her, the truth to which she listened, the truth for which she longed, the truth for which she sighed. Hungering for the truth she ate it, thirsting she drank it. She ate him to whom she listened.[2]

---

1. Benedict Rogers, *From Burma to Rome* (Leominster: Gracewing, 2015), pp. 99–100.
2. St Augustine, *Sermon 179, 4.*

Indeed, as God has provided bread for our bodies, he has also provided bread for our souls: the living bread, the true manna, Christ Jesus himself. Just as we feed on the word of God in the Scriptures, so we feed on the Word of God in Holy Communion. As the Word of God was made flesh in the Incarnation, the bread becomes this flesh, risen and glorified, at the consecration of the Mass. Instituted at the Last Supper on the night he was betrayed, the Eucharist is Christ's gift of love "to the end" (John 13:1), a love without end, unconquered by death, a love which transformed death into a life-giving sacrifice of redemption. By our partaking of this sacred and sacrificial banquet which fulfils and far surpasses all the sacrificial meals of the Old Testament, we receive this gift of our Redeemer's love and deepen our participation in the divine life given to us in Baptism. Our Lord becomes our food for the journey, our companion on the way. He abides in us and we in him, our life, our hope, our joy.[3]

Moreover, Holy Communion is a pledge and foretaste of the heavenly banquet, the marriage supper of the Lamb, the eternal, blissful communion of the soul with God, in an unending feast of love.[4]

---

3. There is discussion among scholars as to the exact meaning of the Greek word *epiousios*—usually translated as daily, "our daily bread"—as this was the first use of the word in Greek literature. It has been reasonably argued that it actually means *supernatural* or *supersubstantial* bread, which is how St Jerome translated it in the Vulgate and which still appears in the Douay Rheims Bible. In that case, this line of the Our Father is fundamentally a prayer for the bread of the Eucharist, the food of everlasting life. cf. Brant Pitre, *Jesus and the Jewish Roots of the Eucharist* (New York: Image, 2016), pp. 93–96.

4. For an elucidation of the nuptial imagery used in the Bible, see Brant Pitre, *Jesus the Bridegroom* (New York: Image, 2014).

Come then, good Shepherd, bread divine
Still show to us thy mercy sign;
Oh, feed us still, still keep us thine;
So that we see thy glories shine
    In the fields of immortality;
O thou, the wisest, mightiest, best,
Our present food, our future rest,
Come, make us each thy chosen guest,
Co-heirs of thine, and comrades blest
    With saints whose dwelling is with thee. Amen.[5]

5.   Conclusion of the Sequence for the feast of Corpus Christi, *Lauda Sion*, attributed to St Thomas Aquinas.

Subheadings of the Biblical meditation which follows

• God gives us nourishment through his creation and providence.

• We are encouraged to pray for our needs, acknowledging our dependence on God.

• Man is also expected to work for his daily bread.

• We are to be content with what is sufficient, without greed.

• We are asked to be generous to help those in need.

• God can also provide food miraculously.

• God's word, wisdom and will are spiritual nourishment

• These themes converge and culminate in the Eucharist, Christ's gift of himself as food for our souls.

• Appearances of the risen Lord with Eucharistic resonances.

• The Eucharistic breaking of bread immediately became part of the life of the early Church.

• The Eucharist foreshadows the heavenly banquet, the marriage feast of the Lamb.

God gives us nourishment through his creation and providence

Genesis 1:29

And God said, "Behold, I have given you every plant yielding seed which is upon the face of all the earth, and every tree with seed in its fruit; you shall have them for food."

Genesis 9:3

Every moving thing that lives shall be food for you; and as I gave you the green plants, I give you everything.

Psalm 145(144):15–16

> The eyes of all look to thee,
>> and thou givest them their food in due season.
> Thou openest thy hand,
>> thou satisfiest the desire of every living thing.

Acts 14:17

He [God] did not leave himself without witness, for he did good and gave you from heaven rains and fruitful seasons, satisfying your hearts with food and gladness.

We are encouraged to pray for our needs acknowledging our dependence on God

Matthew 7:7, 9–11

Ask and it will be given to you; seek and you will find; knock and it will be opened to you ... or what man of you, if his son asks him for bread, will give him a stone? Or if he asks for a fish, will give him a serpent? If you then, who are evil, know how to give good gifts to your children, how much more will your father who us in heaven give good things to those who ask him!

Philippians 4:6

Have no anxiety about anything, but in everything by prayer and supplication with thanksgiving let your requests be made known to God.

Philippians 4:19

My God will supply every need of yours according to his riches in glory in Christ Jesus.

Man is also expected to work for his daily bread

Genesis 3:17–19

> To Adam he said,
> "Because you have listened to the voice of your wife,
>   and have eaten of the tree
> of which I commanded you,
>   'You shall not eat of it.'
> cursed is the ground because of you;
>   in toil you shall eat of it all the days of your life;
> thorns and thistles it shall bring forth to you;
>   and you shall eat the plants of the field,
> in the sweat of your face
>   you shall eat bread
> till you return to the ground."

2 Thessalonians 3:7–8

You yourselves know how you ought to imitate us; we were not idle when we were with you, we did not eat any one's bread without paying, but with toil and labour we worked night and day, that we might not burden any of you.

2 Thessalonians 3:10–12

We gave you this command: If any one will not work, let him not eat. For we hear that some of you are living in idleness, mere busybodies, not doing any work. Now such persons we command and exhort in the Lord Jesus Christ to do their work in quietness and to earn their own living.

We are to be content with what is sufficient, without greed

Luke 12:15–21

He [Jesus] said to them, "Take heed, and beware of all covetousness; for a man's life does not consist in the abundance of his possessions." And he told them a parable, saying, "The land of a rich man brought forth plentifully; and he thought to himself, 'What shall I do, for I have no-where to store my crops?' And he said, 'I will do this: I will pull down my barns, and build larger ones; and then I will store all my grain and my goods. And I will say to my soul, Soul, you have ample goods laid up for many years; take your ease, eat, drink and be merry.' But God said to him, 'Fool! This night your soul is required of you; and the things you have prepared, whose will they be?' So is he who lays up treasure for himself, and is not rich toward God."

1 Timothy 6:6–8

There is great gain in godliness with contentment; for we brought nothing into the world, and we cannot take any-thing out of the world; but if we have food and clothing, with these we shall be content.

We are asked to be generous to help those in need

Deuteronomy 15:11

The poor will never cease out of the land; therefore I command you, You shall open wide your hand to your brother, to the needy and to the poor, in the land.

Tobit 4:7–8

Give alms from your possessions to all who live uprightly, and do not let your eye begrudge the gift when you make it. Do not turn your face away from any poor man, and the face of God will not be turned away from you. If you have many possessions, make your gift from them in proportion; if few, do not be afraid to give according to the little you have.

Luke 16:19–23

There was a rich man, who was clothed in purple and fine linen and who feasted sumptuously every day. And at his gate lay a poor man named Lazarus, full of sores, who desired to be fed with what fell from the rich man's table; moreover the dogs came and licked his sores. The poor man died and was carried by the angels to Abraham's bosom. The rich man also died and was buried; in Hades, being in torment, he lifted up his eyes, and saw Abraham far off and Lazarus in his bosom.

2 Corinthians 9:8, 10–11

God is able to provide you with every blessing in abundance, so that you may always have enough of everything and may provide in abundance for every good work … He who supplies seed to the sower and bread for food will supply and multiply your resources and increase the harvest of your righteousness. You will be enriched in every way for great generosity, which through us will produce thanksgiving to God.

God can also provide food miraculously

Exodus 16:14–15, 21

When the dew had gone up, there was on the face of the wilderness a fine, flake-like thing, fine as hoarfrost on the ground. When the people of Israel saw it, they said to one another, "What is it?" For they did not know what it was. And Moses said to them, "It is the bread which the Lord has given you to eat" ... Morning by morning they gathered it, each as much as he could eat.

1 Kings 19:5–8

He [Elijah] lay down and slept under a broom tree; and behold an angel touched him, and said to him, "Arise and eat." And he looked, and behold, there was at his head a cake baked on hot stones and a jar of water. And he ate and drank, and lay down again. And the angel of the Lord came again a second time, and touched him and said, "Arise and eat, else the journey will be too great for you." And he arose, and ate and drank, and went in the strength of that food forty days and forty nights to Horeb, the mount of God.

2 Kings 4:42–44

A man came from Baal-shalishah, bringing the man of God bread of the first fruits, twenty loaves of barley, and fresh ears of grain in his sack. And Elisha said, "Give to the men, that they may eat." But his servant said, "How am I to set this before a hundred men?" So he repeated, "Give them to the men, that they may eat, for thus says the LORD, 'They shall eat and have some left.'" So he set it before them. And they ate, and had some left, according to the word of the LORD.

Matthew 15:32–37

Then Jesus called his disciples to him and said, "I have compassion on the crowd, because they have been with me now three days, and have nothing to eat; and I am unwilling to send them away hungry, lest they faint on the way." And his disciples said to him, "Where are we to get bread enough in the desert to feed so great a crowd?" And Jesus said to them, "How many loaves have you?" They said, "Seven, and a few small fish." And commanding the crowd to sit down on the ground, he took the seven loaves and the fish, and having given thanks, he broke them and gave them to the disciples, and the disciples gave them to the crowds. And they all ate and were satisfied.

God's word, wisdom and will are spiritual nourishment

Deuteronomy 8:3

He humbled you and let you hunger and fed you with manna which you did not know, nor did your fathers know; that he might make you know that man does not live by bread alone, but that man lives by everything that proceeds out of the mouth of the Lord.

Jeremiah 15:16

> Thy words were found, and I ate them,
> and thy words became to me a joy
> and the delight of my heart.

Sirach 15:1, 3

> and he who holds to the law will obtain wisdom ...
> She will feed him with the bread of understanding,
> and give him the water of wisdom to drink.

John 4:32–34

"I have food to eat of which you do not know." So the disciples said to one another, "Has anyone brought him food?" Jesus said to them, "My food is to do the will of him who sent me, and to accomplish his work."

These themes converge and culminate in the Eucharist, Christ's gift of himself as food for our souls

John 6:27

Do not labour for the food which perishes, but for the food which endures to eternal life, which the Son of man will give to you.

John 6:31–35

"Our fathers ate the manna in the wilderness: as it is written, 'He gave them bread from heaven to eat.'" Jesus said to them, "Truly, truly, I say to you, it was not Moses who gave you the bread from heaven; my Father gives you the true bread from heaven. For the bread of God is that which comes down from heaven, and gives life to the world." They said to him, "Lord, give us this bread always." Jesus said to them, "I am the bread of life; he who comes to me shall not hunger, and he who believes in me shall never thirst."

John 6:55–58

My flesh is food indeed, and my blood is drink indeed. He who eats my flesh and drinks my blood abides in me and I in him. As the living Father sent me, and I live because of the Father, so he who eats me will live because of me. This is the bread which came down from heaven, not such as the fathers ate and died; he who eats this bread will live for ever.

Luke 22:19

He took bread, and when he had given thanks he broke it and gave it to them, saying, "This is my body which is given for you. Do this in remembrance of me."

Appearances of the risen Lord with Eucharistic resonances

Luke 24:30–31, 35

When he was at table with them, he took the bread and blessed, and broke it, and gave it to them. And their eyes were opened and they recognised him; and he vanished out of their sight ... Then they told what had happened on the road, and how he was known to them in the breaking of the bread.

John 21:13–14

Jesus came and took the bread and gave it to them, and so with the fish. This was now the third time that Jesus was revealed to the disciples after he was raised from the dead.

The Eucharistic breaking of bread immediately became part of the life of the early Church

Acts 2:42, 46–47

They devoted themselves to the apostles' teaching and fellowship, to the breaking of bread and the prayers ... And day by day, attending the temple together and breaking bread in their homes, they partook of food with glad and generous hearts, praising God and having favour with all the people.

1 Corinthians 10:16–17

The bread which we break, is it not a participation in the body of Christ? Because there is one bread, we who are many are one body, for we all partake of the one bread.

The Eucharist foreshadows the heavenly banquet, the marriage feast of the Lamb

Isaiah 25:6, 8

On this mountain, the Lord of hosts will make for all peoples a feast of fat things, a feast of wine on the lees, of fat things full of marrow, of wine on the lees well refined ... He will swallow up death for ever, and the Lord God will wipe away tears from all faces.

Luke 22:29–30

As my Father appointed a kingdom for me, so do I appoint for you that you may eat and drink at my table in my kingdom.

Revelation 19:6–7, 9

"Hallelujah! For the Lord our God the almighty reigns.
Let us rejoice and exult and give him the glory,
for the marriage of the Lamb has come,
and his Bride has made herself ready" ...
And the angel said to me, "Write this: Blessed are those
who are invited to the marriage supper of the Lamb."

VI

And Forgive us our Trespasses as we Forgive those who Trespass against us

Be pleased, O Lord,
with these sacrificial offerings,
and grant that we who beseech pardon
for our own sins,
may take care to forgive our neighbour.

Prayer over the Offerings, 3rd Sunday of Lent

We are all sinners. As we have seen, the original sin of our first parents—choosing self-will in preference to God and his will—damaged human nature, leaving it alienated from God and ever prone to sin. It was defined at the Council of Trent that, although with the help of grace it is possible to avoid all mortal sin, we cannot avoid all venial sin except by a special privilege of God, as in the case of the Blessed Virgin Mary.[1] Everyone, from the greatest saint to the greatest sinner, is, therefore, utterly dependent on the forgiveness of God. We have no righteousness of our own.

The Old Testament is full of sins; nothing is glossed over. Immediately after Moses had received the Ten Commandments from God and the people had sworn to obey

---

1.   Cf. Denzinger-Schönmetzer, *Enchiridion Symbolorum*, 1573 (Barcelona: Herder, 1976), p. 380.

him, they turned away, made a golden calf and sacrificed to it (Exodus 32). Through Moses' intercession, God's anger was appeased. There followed a second proclamation of his name: "The Lord, the Lord ... a God merciful and gracious, slow to anger and abounding in steadfast love and faithfulness" (Exodus 34:6). There would be much need of recourse to this mercy.

The prophets, speaking in the name of God, repeatedly urged the chosen people to repent, to turn back to the Lord, to amend their ways, to be true to the covenant. There were elaborate rituals and sacrifices for purification and reparation laid down in the Law of Moses, detailed particularly in the book of Leviticus. These culminated in the annual Day of Atonement (16; 23:26–32) when the high priest offered a bull for himself and his house, and a goat for the whole people of Israel, in atonement for their sins. He entered the holy of holies and sprinkled the blood on the mercy seat and afterwards on the altar, and then confessed all the sins of the people over the scapegoat which bore all their iniquities out into the wilderness. "And this shall be an everlasting statute for you, that atonement may be made for the people of Israel once in the year because of all their sins" (16:34).

These rituals and sacrifices were instituted by the Lord himself. They were intended to teach the people to offer worship to the one, true God, to acknowledge his sovereignty, to confess and to ask forgiveness for their sins. Yet he protested through the prophets that ritual offerings were useless without real compunction of heart and sorrow for sin: "For I desire steadfast love and not sacrifice, the knowledge of God, rather than burnt offerings" (Hosea 6:6. See also Isaiah 1). This was understood by the psalmist, "For thou hast no delight in sacrifice; were I to give a burnt offering, thou wouldst not be pleased. The sacrifice acceptable to God is a broken spirit; a broken and contrite heart, O God, thou wilt not despise" (51(50):16–17).

The letter to the Hebrews asserts that these prescriptions of the Law were a mere shadow of the true form which was to come, and were not efficacious for the expiation of sin, "For it is impossible that the blood of bulls and goats should take away sins" (10:4). They were a preparation, a form of pedagogy for the true sacrifice which really would take away all the sins of the world— the death of Christ on the Cross. The words of Psalm 40(39):6–8 are put on his lips:

> Sacrifices and offerings thou hast not desired, but a body has thou prepared for me; in burnt offerings and sin offerings thou hast taken no pleasure. Then I said, "Lo, I have come to do thy will, O God," as it is written of me in the roll of the book (10:5–7).

The letter continues, "When Christ had offered for all time a single sacrifice for sins, he sat down at the right hand of God ... For by a single offering he has perfected for all time those who are sanctified" (10:12, 14).

Christ was both priest and victim on the altar of the Cross, the Lamb of God offering his death for the salvation of the world. His blood has replaced the blood of animals; he is the true "mercy seat," God's presence Incarnate, the expiation for sins. This offering fulfilled and replaced all the ritual of the Day of Atonement. Yet to kill the Incarnate Son of God was the worst sin that could ever be committed. How could good come of it? He, the sinless One, the only innocent member of our race, the second Adam, burned up all the hatred and evil which crucified him in the fire of his human and divine love. By forgiving those who put him to death—which includes all of us, since we have all sinned and Jesus bore the sins of all time—and by freely offering his suffering and death in reparation to his Father, the greatest possible good was achieved: man was reconciled to God.

While acknowledging that the mystery of the Cross will always transcend human reason, Pope Benedict, nevertheless, offers insights:

> Again and again people say: It must be a cruel God who demands infinite atonement. Is this not a notion unworthy of God? ... The reality of evil and injustice that disfigures the world and at the same time distorts the image of God—this really exists, through our sin. It cannot simply be ignored, it must be addressed. But here it is not a case of a cruel God demanding the infinite. It is exactly the opposite: God himself becomes the locus of reconciliation, and in the person of his Son takes the suffering upon himself. God himself grants his infinite purity to the world. God himself "drinks the cup" of every horror to the dregs and thereby restores justice through the greatness of his love, which, through suffering, transforms the darkness.[2]

How do we apply Christ's saving work to ourselves? How do we have our own sins forgiven? In the first place, through faith and Baptism. Baptism had already been foretold in the book of Ezekiel:

> I will sprinkle clean water upon you, and you shall be clean from all your uncleannesses, and from all your idols I will cleanse you. A new heart I will give you, and a new spirit I will put within you ... And I will put my spirit within you, and cause you to walk in my statutes and be careful to observe my ordinances (36:25–27).

St Paul links Baptism with the death and Resurrection of Christ in this way:

2.   Pope Benedict, *Jesus of Nazareth Part Two*, p. 232.

> Do you not know that all of us who have been
> baptized into Christ Jesus were baptized into his
> death? We were buried therefore with him by
> baptism into death, so that as Christ was raised
> from the dead by the glory of the Father, we too
> might walk in newness of life ... We know that our
> old self was crucified with him, so that the sinful
> body might be destroyed, and we might no longer
> be enslaved to sin (Romans 6:3–4, 6).

This forms part of the reading at the Easter Vigil, shortly before the conferring of Baptism and/or the renewal of Baptismal promises. As the Catechism states, "By Baptism *all sins* are forgiven, original sin and all personal sins, as well as punishment for sins."[3] It infuses grace, the life of God, into our soul.

We are left, however, to wrestle with concupiscence, that inclination to sin, which is a consequence of original sin. The dividing line between good and evil passes through the heart of each one of us. We all bear within us the seeds of the seven deadly or capital sins: pride, avarice, envy, anger, lust, gluttony and sloth. We aim to walk worthily as children of God, led by the Spirit and pleasing to him, but the just man falls seven times a day. Our Lord must stoop daily to wash our feet even when we have been bathed.

His unique sacrifice is made present and efficacious every day on the altar when holy Mass is offered. It is not a repetition of the sacrifice, as was necessary in the Old Testament. It is the same, one and only redemptive sacrifice offered anew for the salvation of the living and the dead. "Grant us, O Lord, we pray, that we may participate worthily in these mysteries, for whenever the memorial of this sacrifice is celebrated the work of our

---

3.   *CCC* 1263.

redemption is accomplished."[4] To be present at Mass is to be present at Calvary. Many of the Prayers over the Offerings pray that this sacrifice may be availing for us: "Grant us, Lord, we pray, a sincere respect for your gifts, that, through the purifying action of your grace, we may be cleansed by the very mysteries we serve."[5] In addition, we acknowledge our sinfulness in the Penitential Rite, we ask the Lamb of God to have mercy on us before Holy Communion, and the worthy reception of Our Lord in this sacrament is itself a remedy for our venial sins.

We can also ask forgiveness by praying the Our Father, by an act of contrition, by signing ourselves with holy water and by acts of charity, for love covers a multitude of sins. Moreover, let us not overlook the value and efficacy of a simply apology to those we have wronged.

The most precious means, however, for the forgiveness of sins after Baptism—especially the most serious ones— is sacramental confession. We are obliged to confess all mortal sins, that is, grave violations of the law of God, committed with full knowledge and full consent of our will. Such sins kill the life of God within us and, if not repented, lead to eternal death.

Confession is also recommended for lesser, daily faults, as being the best means of uprooting the underlying causes of our sins, of renewing our sorrow and resolve to amend, and of strengthening our resistance to temptation. To name our sins and acknowledge them to another who acts in the name of Christ, and to be sure of God's forgiveness, is liberating, enabling us to make a fresh start: "I absolve you from your sins ... Go in peace." We can also

---

4.   Prayer over the Offerings, Mass of the Lord's Supper on Maundy Thursday and 2nd Sunday of the Year.
5.   Prayer over the Offerings, 29th Sunday of the Year.

benefit from the counsel and encouragement a priest may give us.

Many saints practised weekly confession. Regular reception of this sacrament prevents sin from becoming ingrained and less repugnant to us. It keeps the eyes of our heart full of light to see where we fail and whither God is calling us; "Friend, go up higher" (Luke 14:10). It maintains a healthy conscience, for as St John Henry Newman points out:

> Conscience at first warns us against sin; but if we disregard it, it soon ceases to upbraid us; and thus sins, once known, in time become secret sins. It seems then (and it is a startling reflection), that the more guilty we are, the less we know it; for the oftener we sin, the less we are distressed at it. I think many of us may, on reflection, recollect instances, in our experience of ourselves, of our gradually forgetting things to be wrong which once shocked us. Such is the force of habit.[6]

He continues:

> Now what is the chief guide amid the evil and seducing customs of the world?—obviously, the Bible. "The world passeth away, but the word of the Lord endureth for ever" (Isaiah 40:8) ... Our conscience gets corrupted—true; but the words of truth, though effaced from our minds, remain in Scripture, bright in their eternal youth and purity. Yet we do not study Scripture to stir up and refresh our minds.[7]

Let us prove him wrong at least on that point!

Our sins are not merely the breaking of a regulation, but a wound in the heart of Christ. The more deliberate and ma-

---

6.   St John Henry Newman, *PS.* I, 4, "Secret Faults," p. 51.
7.   *Ibid.,* p. 53.

licious they are, the more they add to his sufferings on the Cross. That is the immense price that has been paid for the forgiveness of our sins; confessing our sins is the small price that we have to pay to avail ourselves of that forgiveness.

There is a condition, however, as laid down in the second half of this petition of the Lord's Prayer: "Forgive us our trespasses *as we forgive those who trespass against us.*" Our Lord emphasizes its importance by repeating and expanding it at the end of the prayer. "For if you forgive men their trespasses, your heavenly Father also will forgive you; but if you do not forgive men their trespasses, neither will your Father forgive your trespasses" (Matthew 6:14–15). Our eternal salvation depends upon our forgiveness of others. We cannot have our own sins forgiven while deliberately refusing mercy to our neighbour. We cannot enter heaven with an unforgiving heart or with private enmities. Sr Lucia, one of the seers at Fatima, speaks firmly about this:

> As we see, we cannot obtain God's pardon unless we ourselves first forgive our brothers and sisters. It follows that we must not harbour resentment, ill-will, dislike, and still less a desire to avenge any offence, whether great or small, that one or other of our neighbours may have committed against us. Our forgiveness must be generous, complete and self-sacrificing, in the sense of overcoming ourselves. It will be necessary to silence within us the cry of revolt, to calm excited nerves, to keep a firm grasp on the reins of our own temper and keep a lid on the heat of our wounded self-love which, whether rightly or wrongly, feels bruised and irritated.[8]

"Let the peace of Christ rule in your hearts" (Colossians 3:15). It is only by the power of grace, by the Holy Spirit dwelling

---

8.   Sister Lucia, *"Calls" from the Message of Fatima* (Fatima: Secretariado dos Pastorinhos, 2000), p. 87.

within us, that we can practise forgiveness. Reception of the sacraments, meditation on Scripture, and prayer—particularly in the presence of the Blessed Sacrament—help to establish our hearts in that peace which enables us to be at peace with others, for emotional pain is more effectively assuaged not by resistance but by being accepted and taken to Our Lord. When all else fails, the prayer of desperation, "Lord, I'm helpless; please do something," is always answered.

"Father, forgive them." Jesus asks us to follow in his footsteps, to be united with him and do what he did on the Cross: to have a love stronger than the sin which assails us. It can demand heroic virtue. We can humble our pride and egoism, our tendency to take ourselves too seriously, in order to pass over daily slights—real or imagined—which we, after all, also inflict on others. Such offences as adultery, abandonment, rape, violence, exploitation and murder are in a different category. Nevertheless, secular psychology is at one with Christianity in proclaiming the need to forgive even these, for our mental as well as our spiritual health. We prolong the damage that has been done to us by harbouring bitterness. Interior negativity is destructive; it can ruin our life.[9] The spiritual journey towards peace can be long, as initially we might lack even the slightest desire to forgive. Kathleen Beckman writes candidly of her own experience, following the murder of her father-in-law. The culprits were never found.

> I could not easily move forward after such violent trauma. I felt vulnerable to more violence and murder; nothing felt safe. Fear and anger overcame me. In private, I wept often. I began praying before

---

9. The Church's healing ministry includes such programmes as Grief to Grace for victims of abuse, particularly clerical abuse, and Rachel's Vineyard, for post-abortion trauma.

the Blessed Sacrament for long hours, conversing with Jesus. I expressed anger, "Where were You, Lord? How could You allow this?" I was praying for justice.

After a few weeks, the Lord spoke to my heart: "I want you to pray for the murderers, please." I protested and refused to do so. I remained very unsettled. Each day before the Blessed Sacrament, Jesus spoke to my heart: "I am inviting you to echo my words from the Cross: 'Father, forgive them, for they know not what they are doing.'" I told the Lord that I would say those words but not mean them. Over time, He kept prompting me to repeat His words of forgiveness.

When I finally prayed, in earnest, for the salvation of the souls of the murderers, my peace and joy returned. I was set free. I surrendered justice to God and genuinely hoped that the murderers would not be eternally lost. When I prayed for the murderers' salvation, Jesus flooded my soul with deep awareness of His unfathomable mercy for sinners. I understood that *no one*, even the greatest sinner, is outside God's mercy.[10]

10. Kathleen Beckman, *God's Healing Mercy* (Manchester, NH: Sophia Institute Press, 2015), pp. 35–36.

Subheadings of the Biblical meditation which follows

- God is merciful and forgives sins.
- Calls to repentance in the Old Testament.
- God is always ready to grant pardon, but unrepentant sinners will be punished.
- This teaching is echoed in the New Testament: calls to repentance ...
- ... and warnings of punishment for failure to repent.
- We are urged to acknowledge and confess our sins.
- Confessions of sins.
- Prayers for forgiveness.
- Jesus has the divine authority to forgive sins.
- This authority is given to the Apostles.
- Christ's redemptive death was foretold by Isaiah.
- Jesus shed his blood on the cross for the forgiveness of sins.
- Teaching on forgiveness of others in the Old Testament.
- This teaching exemplified.
- The practice of mercy and forgiveness of others is at the heart of the Gospel.
- Forgiveness in the life and teaching of the early Church.

God is merciful and forgives sins

Sirach 17:29

> How great is the mercy of the Lord,
> and his forgiveness for those who turn to him!

Luke 15:7

I tell you, there will be more joy in heaven over one sinner who repents than over ninety-nine righteous persons who need no repentance.

Calls to repentance in the Old Testament

Sirach 17:25–26

> Turn to the Lord and forsake your sins;
> pray in his presence and lessen your offences.
> Return to the Most High and turn away from iniquity,
> and hate abominations intensely.

Isaiah 55:7

> Let the wicked forsake his way
> and the unrighteous man his thoughts;
> let him return to the Lord, that he may have mercy on him,
> and to our God, for he will abundantly pardon.

Ezekiel 18:30–32

Repent and turn away from all your transgressions, lest iniquity be your ruin. Cast away from you all the transgressions which you have committed against me, and get yourselves a new heart and a new spirit! Why will you die, O house of Israel? For I have no pleasure in the death of any one, says the Lord God; so turn and live.

God is always ready to grant pardon, but unrepentant sinners will be punished

Wisdom 12:2, 26

> Therefore thou dost correct little by little
>   those who trespass,
> and dost remind and warn them
>   of the things wherein they sin,
> that they may be freed from wickedness
>   and put their trust in thee, O Lord ...
> But those who have not heeded
>   the warning of light rebukes
> will experience the deserved judgment of God.

Sirach 5:4–7

> Do not say, "I sinned, and what happened to me?"
>   for the Lord is slow to anger.
> Do not be so confident of atonement
>   that you add sin to sin.
> Do not say, "His mercy is great,
>   he will forgive the multitude of my sins,"
> for both mercy and wrath are with him,
>   and his anger rests on sinners.
> Do not delay to turn to the Lord,
>   nor postpone it from day to day;
> for suddenly the wrath of the Lord will go forth,
>   and at the time of punishment you will perish.

This teaching is echoed in the New Testament: calls to repentance ...

Luke 5:32

I have not come to call the righteous, but sinners to repentance.

Acts 2:37–38

When they heard this they were cut to the heart, and said to Peter and the rest of the apostles, "Brethren, what shall we do?" And Peter said to them, "Repent, and be baptized every one of you in the name of Jesus Christ for the forgiveness of your sins; and you shall receive the gift of the Holy Spirit."

2 Corinthians 5:19–20

God was in Christ reconciling the world to himself, not counting their trespasses against them, and entrusting to us the message of reconciliation. So we are ambassadors for Christ, God making his appeal through us. We beseech you on behalf of Christ, be reconciled to God.

... and warnings of punishment for failure to repent

Matthew 11:20, 24

He began to upbraid the cities where most of his mighty works had been done, because they did not repent ... "I tell you that it shall be more tolerable on the day of judgment for the land of Sodom than for you."

Romans 2:4–6

Do you not know that God's kindness is meant to lead you to repentance? But by your hard and impenitent heart you are storing up wrath for yourself on the day of wrath, when God's righteous judgment will be revealed. For he will render to every man according to his works.

We are urged to acknowledge and confess our sins

James 5:16

Confess your sins to one another, and pray for one another, that you may be healed.

1 John 1:7–10

If we walk in the light, as he is in the light, we have fellowship with one another, and the blood of Jesus his Son cleanses us from all sins. If we say we have no sin, we deceive ourselves, and the truth is not in us. If we confess our sins, he is faithful and just, and will forgive our sins and cleanse us from all unrighteousness. If we say we have not sinned, we make him a liar, and his word is not in us."

Confessions of sins

Psalm 32(31):3–5

When I declared not my sin, my body wasted away
    through my groaning all day long.
For day and night thy hand was heavy upon me;
    my strength was dried up as by the heat of summer.
I acknowledged my sin to thee,
    and I did not hide my iniquity;
I said, "I will confess my transgressions to the Lord";
    then thou didst forgive the guilt of my sin.

Daniel 9:4–6

I prayed to the Lord my God and made confession, saying, "O Lord, the great and terrible God who keeps covenant and steadfast love with those who love him and keep his commandments, we have sinned and done wrong and acted wickedly and rebelled, turning aside from thy commandments and ordinances; we have not listened to thy servants the prophets, who spoke in thy name to our kings, our princes, and our fathers, and to all the people of Israel."

Mark 1:4–5

John the baptizer appeared in the wilderness, preaching a baptism of repentance for the forgiveness of sins. And there went out to him all the country of Judea, and all the people of Jerusalem; and they were baptized by him in the river Jordan, confessing their sins.

Prayers for forgiveness

Psalm 50(51):1–3

Have mercy on me, O God, according to thy steadfast love;
> according to thy abundant mercy blot out my transgressions.

Wash me thoroughly from my iniquity,
> and cleanse me from my sin!

For I know my transgressions,
> and my sin is ever before me.

Daniel 9:18–19

O my God, incline thy ear and hear; open thy eyes and behold our desolations, and the city which is called by thy name; for we do not present our supplications before thee on the ground of our righteousness, but on the ground of thy great mercy. O Lord, hear; O Lord, forgive; O Lord give heed and act; delay not, for thy own sake, O my God, because thy city and thy people are called by thy name.

Luke 18:13

The tax collector, standing far off, would not even lift up his eyes to heaven, but beat his breast, saying, "God be merciful to me a sinner."

Jesus has the divine authority to forgive sins

Matthew 9:2–7

They brought to him a paralytic, lying on his bed; and when Jesus saw their faith he said to the paralytic, "Take heart, my son; your sins are forgiven." And behold, some of the scribes said to themselves, "This man is blaspheming." But Jesus, knowing their thoughts, said, "Why do you think evil in your hearts? For which is easier, to say, 'Your sins are forgiven,' or to say, 'Rise and walk'? But that you may know that the Son of man has authority on earth to forgive sins"—he then said to the paralytic—"Rise, take up your bed and go home." And he rose and went home.

Luke 7: 48–50

He said to her, "Your sins are forgiven." Then those who were at table with him began to say among themselves, "Who is this, who even forgives sins?" And he said to the woman, "Your faith has saved you; go in peace."

This authority is given to the Apostles

John 20: 22–23

Receive the Holy Spirit. If you forgive the sins of any, they are forgiven; if you retain the sins of any, they are retained.

Christ's redemptive death was foretold by Isaiah

Isaiah 53:4–6

> Surely he has borne our griefs
>   and carried our sorrows;
> yet we esteemed him stricken,
>   smitten by God, and afflicted.
> But he was wounded for our transgressions,
>   he was bruised for our iniquities;
> upon him was the chastisement that made us whole,
>   and with his stripes, we are healed.
> All we like sheep have gone astray;
>   we have turned every one to his own way;
> and the Lord has laid on him the iniquity of us all.

Isaiah 53:12

> ... he poured out his soul to death,
>> and was numbered with the transgressors;
> yet he bore the sin of many,
>> and made intercession for the transgressors.

Jesus shed his blood on the cross for the forgiveness of sins

Matthew 26:27–28

He took a cup, and when he had given thanks he gave it to them saying, "Drink of it, all of you; for this is my blood of the covenant, which is poured out for many for the forgiveness of sins."

Romans 3:23–25

Since all have sinned and fall short of the glory of God, they are justified by his grace as a gift, through the redemption which is in Christ Jesus, whom God put forward as an expiation by his blood, to be received by faith.

Colossians 1:19–20

For in him the fullness of God was pleased to dwell, and through him to reconcile to himself all things, whether on earth or in heaven, making peace by the blood of his cross.

Teaching on forgiveness of others in the Old Testament

Sirach 10:6

Do not be angry with your neighbour for any injury.

Sirach 28:1–6

> He that takes vengeance will suffer vengeance from the Lord
>> and he will firmly establish his sins.
> Forgive your neighbour the wrong he has done,

and then your sins will be pardoned when you pray.
Does a man harbour anger against another,
    and yet seek for healing from the Lord?
Does he have no mercy toward a man like himself
    and yet pray for his own sins?
If he himself, being flesh, maintains wrath,
    who will make expiation for his sins?
Remember the end of your life, and cease from
enmity,
    remember devastation and death,
    and be true to the commandments.

This teaching exemplified

Genesis 50:15–21

When Joseph's brothers saw that their father was dead, they said, "It may be that Joseph will take us and pay us back for all the evil which we did to him." So they sent a message to Joseph, saying, "Your father gave his command before he died, 'Say to Joseph, Forgive, I pray you the transgression of your brothers and their sin, because they did evil to you.' And now, we pray you, forgive the transgression of the servants of the God of your father." Joseph wept when they spoke to him. His brothers also came and fell down before him, and said, "Behold, we are your servants." But Joseph said to them, "Fear not, for am I in the place of God? As for you, you meant evil against me; but God meant it for good, to bring it about that many people should be kept alive, as they are today. So do not fear; I will provide for you and your little ones." Thus he reassured them and comforted them.

1 Samuel 24:16–18

Saul lifted up his voice and wept. He said to David, "You are more righteous than I; for you have repaid me good, whereas I have repaid you evil. And you have declared this day how you have dealt well with me, in that you did not kill me when the Lord put me into your hands."

The practice of mercy and forgiveness of others is at the heart of the Gospel

Luke 12:34

And Jesus said, "Father, forgive them, for they know not what they do."

Matthew 5:23–24

If you are offering your gift at the altar, and there remember that your brother has something against you, leave your gift there before the altar and go; first be reconciled to your brother, and then come and offer your gift.

Matthew 18: 21–22

Peter came up and said to him, "Lord, how often shall my brother sin against me, and I forgive him? As many as seven times?" Jesus said to him, "I do not say to you seven times, but seventy times seven."

Matthew 18:32–35

"You wicked servant! I forgave you all that debt because you besought me; and should you not have had mercy on your fellow servant, as I had mercy on you?" And in anger his Lord delivered him to the jailers, till he should pay all his debt. So also my heavenly Father will do to every one of you, if you do not forgive your brother from your heart.

Forgiveness in the life and teaching of the early Church

Acts 7:59–60

As they were stoning Stephen, he prayed, "Lord Jesus, receive my spirit." And he knelt down and cried with a loud voice, "Lord, do not hold this sin against them."

Romans 12: 14, 17–21

Bless those who persecute you; bless and do not curse them. Repay no one evil for evil, but take thought for what is noble in the sight of all. If possible, so far as it depends upon you, live peaceably with all. Beloved, never avenge yourselves, but leave it to the wrath of God; for it is written, "Vengeance is mine, I will repay, says the Lord." No, "if your enemy is hungry, feed him; if he is thirsty, give him drink; for by so doing you will heap burning coals upon his head." Do not be overcome by evil, but overcome evil with good.

Colossians 3:12–13

Put on then, as God's chosen ones, holy and beloved, compassion, kindness, lowliness, meekness and patience, forbearing one another and, if one has a complaint against another, forgiving each other; as the Lord has forgiven you, so you almost must forgive.

VII

And Lead us Not into Temptation

Look upon your servants, O Lord,
and in your goodness
protect with heavenly assistance
those who trust in your mercy.

Prayer over the People, Thursday 4th Week of Lent

T he Catechism tells us how we may understand this petition: "The Greek means both 'do not allow us to enter into temptation', and 'do not let us yield to temptation.'"[1] God does not lead us into sin, but he does allow us, indeed wants us, to be tried. "Through many tribulations we must enter the kingdom of God" (Acts 14:22).

Abraham was tested by him in the most demanding way: "Take your son, your only son Isaac, whom you love, and go to the land of Moriah and offer him there as a burnt offering upon one of the mountains" (Genesis 22:2). Abraham obeyed, though he was finally spared from having to carry out the dread deed. "Do not lay your hand on the boy or do anything to him; for now I know that you fear God, seeing you have not withheld your son, your only son, from me" (Genesis 22:12). This obedience was rewarded by great blessings.

---

1.   *CCC* 2846.

God wants to prove our fidelity; Satan wants us to fall away from God. Our first parents were given a test and failed it. Despite the fact that resistance to temptation has been made more difficult by the first Fall as St Paul observes, man still has a choice:

> The Lord said to Cain, "Why are you angry, and why has your countenance fallen? If you do well, will you not be accepted? And if you do not do well, sin is crouching at the door; its desire is for you, but you must master it" (Genesis 4:6–7).

By undergoing trials and mastering temptation, the soul grows in strength and stature, as St Augustine asserts:

> Life for us, as we journey on, must indeed have its testing times, for by their means we make progress, learning our true worth by being put to the test. There can be no crown without victory, no victory without contest, no contest without adversary and testing.[2]

The greater the virtue, the more the devil will rage, as the lives of such saints as St Anthony of Egypt, St Benedict and St Teresa of Avila attest. Most of us won't meet the devil in person but do battle with him we must. "Be sober, be watchful. Your adversary the devil prowls around like a roaring lion, seeking someone to devour. Resist him, firm in your faith" (1 Peter 5:8–9).

Our Lord has gone before us, leading the way. "Jesus, full of the Holy Spirit, returned from the Jordan and was led by the Spirit for forty days in the wilderness, tempted by the devil" (Luke 4:1). St Augustine underlines the unity of Christ with all the members in his body, the Church. This is the whole Christ. We were present in him, therefore, when he was tempted by Satan:

2.   St Augustine, *Commentaries on the Psalms*, Psalm 60, 3.

> In Christ, you also were tempted, since he took to
> himself human nature from you, and salvation
> came to you from him ... In your flesh, then, he
> allowed himself to be tested, and in him you were
> victorious. If in Christ we are put to the test, in him
> we overcome the devil ... See yourself being put to
> the test in him, then see yourself gaining the
> mastery with him. He could have forbidden the
> devil to assail him; but if he had not allowed him-
> self to be tempted, he could not have shown you
> how to conquer in your time of trial.[3]

Jesus shows us how to conquer by using the words of
Scripture to refute the Evil One: when tempted to use his
miraculous power to feed himself, "Man shall not live by
bread alone" (Deuteronomy 8:3); when tempted to worship Satan for the sake of earthly power, "You shall
worship the Lord your God and him only shall you serve"
(Deuteronomy 6:13); when tempted to perform a dazzling,
dangerous stunt for human glory, "You shall not tempt the
Lord your God" (Deuteronomy 6:16). The more deeply we
make the word of God our own, the stronger our
resistance to temptation will be, like the wise man who
built his house on the rock; it stood firm when buffeted by
storms (cf. Matthew 7:24–25).

"Continue steadfastly in prayer, being watchful in it
with thanksgiving" (Colossians 4:2). Battling alone,
through pride and self-righteousness, we won't endure.
Throwing ourselves on God's mercy and imploring his aid,
distrusting ourselves, but trusting in him, we can stand
firm. "Being watchful" requires a knowledge of ourselves
and our weaknesses, a firm resolve to *agere contra* — to
practise the virtue opposed to the wrongful inclination —
and a determination to avoid occasions of temptation
where possible. If certain people, places or pursuits lead

3.   *Ibid.*

us into sin, then prudence demands our renunciation of them, for we can't expect divine assistance if we wilfully dally with unnecessary danger. However bitter the remedy seems, and however strong the passions, these feelings won't last forever. The reward for this sacrifice will be interior freedom and peace.

"Turn my eyes from looking at vanities," prays the psalmist (Psalm 119(118):37). In Chapter 4 of his Rule, St Augustine pays particular attention to guarding the eyes for the preservation of chastity following Our Lord's own warning that "every one who looks at a woman lustfully has already committed adultery with her in his heart" (Matthew 5:28). It was his wandering eyes which lead King David into both adultery and murder (cf. 2 Samuel 11). "The eye is the lamp of the body. So, if your eye is sound, your whole body will be full of light; but if your eye is not sound, your whole body will be full of darkness" (Matthew 6:22–23).

"Set a guard over my mouth, O Lord, keep watch over the door of my lips! Incline not my heart to any evil" (Ps 141(140):3–4). Sealing the lips and practising a judicious silence will prevent many a sin for, "no human being can tame the tongue — a restless evil, full of deadly poison" (James 3:8). On the other hand, we can also sin by failing to speak at certain times, for example when speaking the truth or confessing our faith would not be socially acceptable. At such times, we can remember the words of Jesus, "Whoever is ashamed of me and my words in this adulterous and sinful generation, of him will the Son of man also be ashamed, when he comes in the glory of his Father with the holy angels" (Mark 8:38).

Guarding the heart is the primary battleground, "For out of the heart come evil thoughts, murder, adultery, fornication, theft, false witness, slander" (Matthew 15:19). Exposing temptations and our inner demons to a confessor or spiritual guide is recommended by all the spiritual masters, for the devil loves darkness and flees from the light.

The beginning of temptation is a crucial time, for a seedling is more easily uprooted than a sapling:

> We must watch, especially in the beginning of temptation, for then the enemy is more easily overcome, if he be not suffered to enter the door of the mind, but is withstood upon the threshold the very moment that he knocketh ... For first there cometh into the mind a simple thought; then a strong imagination; afterwards delight and the evil motion and consent. And so, by little and little, the malignant foe doth gain full entrance, when he is not resisted in the beginning.[4]

Fighting the thoughts directly is not advised, for what is resisted in this way tends to persist. Turning the mind away is a more effective tactic:

> There is no need to set oneself in opposition to the thoughts. It is better to take refuge in God. If we refrain from fighting the thoughts sown in us by the devil, and in prayer to God break off all contact with them ... we have mastered the shortest route.[5]

The Cloud of Unknowing has these picturesque strategies:

> You are to do all that in you lies to act as though you did not know that they [sinful thoughts] are pressing very hard upon you and coming between you and your God. Try to look over their shoulders as it were, as though you were looking for some-

---

4.   Thomas a Kempis, *The Imitation of Christ*, I, 13 (Leeds: Laverty & Sons, Ltd 1957), p. 42.

5.   Isaac of Nineveh (also known as Isaac the Syrian), *Ascetic Treatises*, 33.

thing else; that something else is God, surrounded on all sides by the cloud of unknowing. If you do this, I am sure that within a short time, you will find your burden easier ... There is another device, which you can put to the test if you so wish. When you feel that you can in no way put down these thoughts, cower down under them like a poor wretch and a coward overcome in battle, and reckon it to be a waste of time for you to strive any longer against them. In this way, though you are in the hands of your enemies, you give yourself up to God; feel as though you were hopelessly defeated.[6]

This device, the author of the Cloud maintains, "is nothing else but a true knowledge and experience of yourself as you are." This experience of oneself as nothingness is humility, and it is precisely this humility — an awareness that of ourselves we can do nothing — that God wants us to learn through undergoing trials and temptations.

This humility merits to have God himself coming down in his power to avenge you against your enemies, to take you up, to cherish you and to dry your spiritual eyes, as the father does for the child that was in danger of death under the mouths of wild boars or mad, biting bears.[7]

Another way of expressing this humility and throwing ourselves on God is to use short prayers from Scripture, such as: "Lord, save me" (Matthew 14:30); "Have mercy on me, O God" (Psalm 51(50):1). While a tempest rages, within or without, we can use Our Lord's words to the storm at sea, "Peace! Be still!" (Mark 4:39).

John Cassian, an influential monk of the fourth-fifth

---

6. Anonymous, *The Cloud of Unknowing, 32* (New York: Paulist Press, 1981), pp. 180–181.

7. *Ibid.*

centuries, passed on the tradition of using the verse, "O God, come to my assistance; O Lord, make haste to help me" (Psalm 69:2),[8] in all circumstances:

> Not without reason has this verse been selected from out of the whole body of Scripture. For it takes up all the emotions that can be applied to human nature and with great correctness and accuracy it adjusts itself to every condition and every attack. It contains an invocation of God in the face of any crisis, the humility of a devout confession, the watchfulness of concern and of constant fear, a consciousness of one's own frailty, the assurance of being heard, and confidence in a protection that is always present and at hand , for whoever calls unceasingly on his protector is sure that he is always present. It contains a burning love and charity, an awareness of traps, and a fear of enemies. Seeing oneself surrounded by these day and night, one confesses that one cannot be set free without the help of one's defender. This verse is an unassailable wall, an impenetrable breastplate, and a very strong shield for all those who labor under the attack of demons.[9]

"The Lord is near to all who call upon him" (Ps 145(144):18), and he never abandons those who trust in him.

---

8.   Douay Rheims Bible.
9.   John Cassian, *The Conferences*, X, 3–4 (New York: Paulist Press, 1997), p. 379.

Subheadings of the Biblical meditation which follows

- God's testing of us in an intrinsic part of human life. Rebellion through pride is the fundamental temptation, aided and abetted by sensuality.
- Trials are intended to prove our fidelity and strengthen our virtue.
- Thanksgiving and joyful acceptance of such trials, recognising their positive value.
- Satan's power is limited by God.
- Jesus was tried and tempted for our sake.
- The battle within ourselves as a result of original sin.
- The world is also a source of temptation.
- God assists us in our temptations.
- Living by the Holy Spirit.
- Exhortations to vigilance, prayer and faith.
- Receptivity to the word of God and perseverance in it will guard the heart.
- Pride will lead us into temptation.
- Our Lord uses strong language to urge us to avoid occasions of sin.
- To lead others into sin is a grave evil.

God's testing of us in an intrinsic part of human life. Rebellion through pride is the fundamental temptation, aided and abetted by sensuality

Genesis 2:16–17

The Lord God commanded the man saying, "You may eat freely of every tree of the garden; but of the tree of the knowledge of good and evil you shall not eat, for in the day that you eat of it you shall die."

Genesis 3:4–6

But the serpent said to the woman, "You shall not die. For God knows that when you eat of it your eyes will be opened, and you will be like God, knowing good and evil." So when the woman saw that the tree was good for food, and that it was a delight to the eyes, and that the tree was to be desired to make one wise, she took of its fruit and ate; and she also gave some to her husband, and he ate.

Trials are intended to prove our fidelity and strengthen our virtue

Sirach 2:1–5

My son, if you come forward to serve the Lord,
    prepare yourself for temptation.
 Set your heart right and be steadfast,
    and do not be hasty in time of calamity.
Cleave to him and do not depart,
    that you may be honoured at the end of your life.
Accept whatever is brought upon you,
    and in changes that humble you be patient.
For gold is tested in the fire,
    and acceptable men in the furnace of humiliation.

Wisdom 3:1, 5–6

> The souls of the righteous are in the hand of God,
>> and no torment will ever touch them ...
>
> Having been disciplined a little, they will receive great good,
> because God tested them and found them worthy of himself;
>> like gold in the furnace he tried them,
>> and like a sacrificial burnt offering he accepted them.

James 1:12

Blessed is the man who endures trial, for when he has stood the test he will receive the crown of life which God has promised to those who love him.

Thanksgiving and joyful acceptance of such trials, recognising their positive value

Judith 8:25–27

In spite of everything let us give thanks to the Lord our God, who is putting us to the test as he did our forefathers. Remember what he did with Abraham and how he tested Isaac, and what happened to Jacob ... For he has not tried us with fire, as he did them, to search their hearts, nor has he taken revenge upon us; but the Lord scourges those who draw near to him, in order to admonish them.

Romans 5:3–5

We rejoice in our sufferings, knowing that suffering produces endurance and endurance produces character, and character produces hope, and hope does not disappoint us, because God's love has been poured into our hearts through the Holy Spirit who has been given to us.

James 1:2–4

Count it all joy, my brethren, when you meet various trials, for you know that the testing of your faith produces steadfastness. And let steadfastness have its full effect, that you may be perfect and complete, lacking in nothing.

Satan's power is limited by God

Job 1:8–12

The Lord said to Satan, "Have you considered my servant Job, that there is none like him on the earth, a blameless and upright man, who fears God and turns away from evil?" Then Satan answered the Lord, "Does Job fear God for naught? Hast thou not put a hedge about him and his house and all that he has, on every side? Thou hast blessed the work of his hands, and his possessions have increased in the land. But put forth thy hand now, and touch all that he has and he will curse thee to thy face." And the Lord said to Satan, "Behold, all that he has is in your power; only upon himself do not put forth your hand."

Job 2:3–6

The Lord said to Satan, "Have you considered my servant Job, that there is none like him on the earth, a blameless and upright man, who fears God and turns away from evil? He still holds fast his integrity, although you moved me against him, to destroy him without cause." Then Satan answered the Lord, "Skin for skin! All that a man has he will give for his life. But put forth thy hand now, and touch his bone and his flesh, and he will curse thee to thy face." And the Lord said to Satan, "Behold, he is in your power; only spare his life."

Jesus was tried and tempted for our sake

Hebrews 2:18

Because he himself has suffered and been tempted, he is able to help those who are tempted.

Hebrews 4:15–16

We have not a high priest who is unable to sympathize with our weaknesses, but one who in every respect has been tempted as we are, yet without sinning. Let us then with confidence draw near to the throne of grace that we may receive mercy and find grace to help in time of need.

Hebrews 12:1–4

Since we are surrounded by so great a cloud of witnesses, let us lay aside every weight, and sin which clings so closely, and let us run with perseverance the race that is set before us, looking to Jesus the pioneer and perfecter of our faith, who for the joy that was set before him endured the cross, despising the shame, and is seated at the right hand of the throne of God. Consider him who endured from sinners such hostility against himself, so that you may not grow weary or fainthearted. In your struggle against sin you have not yet resisted to the point of shedding your blood.

The battle within ourselves as a result of original sin

James 1:13–15

Let no one say when he is tempted, "I am tempted by God"; for God cannot be tempted with evil and he himself tempts no one; but each person is tempted when he is lured and enticed by his own desire. Then desire when it has conceived gives birth to sin; and sin when it is full-grown brings forth death.

Romans 8:15–20

I do not understand my own actions. For I do not do what I want, but I do the very thing I hate. Now if I do what I do not want, I agree that the law is good. So then it is no longer I that do it, but sin which dwells within me. For I know that nothing good dwells within me, that is, in my flesh. I can will what is right, but I cannot do it. For I do not the good I want, but the evil I do not want is what I do. Now if I do what I do not want, it is no longer I that do it, but sin which dwells within me.

Romans 8:21–25

So I find it to be a law that when I want to do right, evil lies close at hand. For I delight in the law of God, in my inmost self, but I see in my members another law at war with the law of my mind and making me captive to the law of sin which dwells in my members. Wretched man that I am! Who will deliver me from this body of death? Thanks be to God through Jesus Christ our Lord!

The world is also a source of temptation

1 John 2:15–16

Do not love the world or the things in the world. If anyone loves the world, love for the Father is not in him. For all that is in the world, the lust of the flesh and the lust of the eyes and the pride of life, is not of the Father but is of the world.

God assists us in our temptations

Luke 22:31

Simon, Simon, behold Satan demanded to have you, that he might sift you like wheat, but I have prayed for you that your faith may not fail.

1 Corinthians 10:13

No temptation has overtaken you that is not common to man. God is faithful and he will not let you be tempted beyond your strength, but with the temptation will also provide the way of escape, that you may be able to endure it.

2 Corinthians 12:7–9

To keep me from being too elated by the abundance of revelations, a thorn was given me in the flesh, a messenger of Satan, to harass me, to keep me from being too elated. Three times I besought the Lord about this, that it should leave me; but he said to me, "My grace is sufficient for you, for my power is made perfect in weakness."

Living by the Holy Spirit

Romans 8:5–7

Those who live according to the flesh set their minds on the things of the flesh, but those who live according to the Spirit set their minds on the things of the Spirit. To set the mind on the flesh is death, but to set the mind on the Spirit is life and peace. For the mind that is set on the flesh is hostile to God; it does not submit to God's law.

Galatians 5:16–17

Walk by the Spirit, and do not gratify the desires of the flesh. For the desires of the flesh are against the Spirit, and the desires of the Spirit are against the flesh; for these are opposed to each other, to prevent you from doing what you would.

Galatians 6:7–8

God is not mocked, for whatever a man sows, that he will

also reap. For he who sows to his own flesh will from the flesh reap corruption; but he who sows to the Spirit will from the Spirit reap eternal life.

Exhortations to vigilance, prayer and faith

Matthew 26:40–41

He [Jesus] came to the disciples and found them sleeping; and he said to Peter, "So could you not watch with me one hour? Watch and pray that you may not enter into temptation; the spirit indeed is willing, but the flesh is weak."

1 Corinthians 16:13

Be watchful, stand firm in your faith, be courageous, be strong.

1 Thessalonians 5:5–6, 8

You are all sons of light and sons of the day; we are not of the night or of the darkness. So then let us not sleep, as others do, but let us keep awake ... Since we belong to the day, let us be sober, and put on the breast plate of faith and love, and for a helmet the hope of salvation.

Receptivity to the word of God and perseverance in it will guard the heart

Proverbs 4:20–23

My son, be attentive to my words;
   incline your ear to my sayings.
Let them not escape from your sight;
   keep them within your heart.
For they are life to him who finds them,
   and healing to all his flesh.
Keep your heart with all diligence,
   for from it flow the springs of life.

Psalm 118(119):11

> I have laid up thy word in my heart,
>> that I might not sin against thee.

Luke 8:11–15

The parable is this: The seed is the word of God. The ones along the path are those who have heard; then the devil comes and takes away the word from their hearts, that they may not believe and be saved. And the ones on the rock are those who, when they hear the word, receive it with joy; but these have no root, they believe for a while and in time of temptation fall away. And as for what fell among the thorns, they are those who hear, but as they go on their way they are choked by the cares and riches and pleasures of life, and their fruit does not mature. And as for that in the good soil, they are those who, hearing the word, hold it fast in an honest and good heart, and bring forth fruit with patience.

Pride will lead us into temptation

1 Corinthians 10:12

Let anyone who thinks that he stands, take heed lest he fall.

Galatians 6:1

Brethren, if a man is overtaken in any trespass, you who are spiritual should restore him in a spirit of gentleness. Look to yourself, lest you too be tempted.

James 4:6–8

"God opposes the proud but gives grace to the humble." Submit yourselves therefore to God. Resist the devil and he will flee from you. Draw near to God and he will draw near to you. Cleanse your hands, you sinners, and purify your hearts, you men of double mind.

Our Lord uses strong language to urge us to avoid occasions of sin

Matthew 18: 8–9 (cf. Matthew 5:29–30)

If your hand or your foot causes you to sin, cut it off and throw it from you; it is better for you to enter life maimed or lame than with two hands or two feet to be thrown into eternal fire. And if your eye causes you to sin, pluck it out and throw it from you; it is better for you to enter life with one eye than with two eyes to be thrown into the hell of fire.

To lead others into sin is a grave evil

Matthew 18:6

Whoever causes one of these little ones who believe in me to sin, it would be better for him to have a great millstone fastened round his neck and to be drowned in the depth of the sea.

Matthew 18:7

Woe to the world for temptations to sin! For it is necessary that temptations come, but woe to the man by whom the temptation comes!

VIII

But Deliver us from Evil

Far from us drive our deadly foe;
True peace unto us bring;
And through all perils lead us safe
Beneath thy sacred wing.

From the hymn *Veni Creator Spiritus*

In the Old Testament, there is a strong sense that God is our deliverer. The preservation of Noah from the flood was a divine initiative. He protected Joseph through all his trials in order to deliver Israel's sons from famine and kept David safe from all his enemies. He rescued the three young men from the fiery furnace, Daniel from the lion's den, and Susanna from unjust condemnation. The greatest act of deliverance, however, to which the people of Israel always looked back, was the liberation from slavery in Egypt. "I am the Lord, and I will bring you out from under the burden of the Egyptians, and I will deliver you from their bondage and I will redeem you with an outstretched arm and with great acts of judgment" (Exodus 6:6).

The Psalms, such as 105(104) and 107(106), recount God's saving acts and express confidence in his power to deliver both the nation and individuals from the evils which surround them. With the Hebrew preference for concrete rather than abstract terms, God is a rock, a fortress, a shield, a stronghold, a hiding place. He protects the weak and needy, he saves from death. Psalms 91(90) and 121(120) are among those which are peacefully trusting and reassuring. In others, Psalms 55(54) and 74(73), for example, the psalmist, surrounded by enemies and wicked men, makes anguished if confident pleas for deliverance.

The combination of distress and lamentation with trust and praise in a single psalm is a characteristic feature of these prayers. It is a divine lesson: this is how God wants us to pray. The Psalms, like all of Scripture, are the word of God. In using them, therefore, we speak to God as he has taught us, in the words he has given us. Moreover, Christ himself prayed with them; they speak of him and he reveals their deepest meaning. Psalm 22(21), for example, vividly portrays his Passion. He is the just man praying in anguish for deliverance and praising God in anticipation.

In keeping with the rest of the Old Testament, Psalms such as 78(77) and 106(105) do not hide the fact that it was necessary at times for God to refuse deliverance to his wayward people. He used the enmity of other nations to punish the Israelites for their sins of infidelity and their idolatry. Such punishment was intended to be remedial, a saving grace, a means of rescuing them from their own folly, since the worst of all ills would be to fall away from God.

The author of all evil is the devil and this petition of the Our Father could equally be translated, "Deliver us from the Evil One." Satan, an angel who was created good as all of God's creatures, rebelled against his Creator. Thrust out of heaven with all his followers, his malign pleasure consists in enticing as many human souls as possible into his own wretched state of damnation. This is the fundamental evil from which we pray to be delivered and our whole salvation lies in Christ.

"The reason the Son of God appeared was to destroy the works of the devil" (1 John 3:8). Jesus called him, "the ruler of this world" (John 14:30), but he had no power over the obedient One. A significant part of his public life was the casting out of demons, a ministry which has been entrusted to the Church to be continued throughout time in his name.[1]

Through the suffering, death and Resurrection of the Incarnate Son the power of the devil was vanquished:

> Since the children share in flesh and blood, he himself likewise partook of the same nature, that through death he might destroy him who has the power of death, that is, the devil, and deliver all those who through fear of death were subject to lifelong bondage (Hebrews 2:14–15).

There is a delightful depiction, by a monastic author, of Our Lord's harrowing of hell and the dismay of the demons:

> For certain he was dead, and for certain he was overcome. Our champion in the world has been deceived! He did not know that this man was preparing a disaster for hell. Oh this cross which destroys our pleasures and engenders our ruin! The wood enriched us, and now the wood ruins us. This great power, which the people always feared, has perished.[2]

At the Easter Vigil the Exsultet, sung in honour of the paschal candle which is a symbol of the risen Lord, proclaims, "This is the night in which Christ snapped the chains of death and rose conqueror from hell."[3] Jesus could rightly say, "Do not fear those who kill the body but cannot kill the soul" (Matthew 10:28). It is echoed by St. Paul, "O death,

---

1. Cf. Beckman, "Rays of Mercy on People with Diabolical Suffering" in *God's Healing Mercy*, pp. 111–125. This helpful chapter looks at both ordinary and extraordinary spiritual warfare and the arsenal recommended by the church.

2. Eusebius the Gallican, *Homily* 12A, 2.

3. Unofficial translation.

where is thy victory? O death, where is thy sting?" (1 Corinthians 15:55). Although we must all die, and we naturally mourn the earthly loss of loved ones, we have been delivered from eternal death. Those who have faith in Christ and keep his word have "passed from death to life" (John 5:24). He warned his disciples that they would be hated on his account, persecuted and killed, "But not a hair of your head will perish. By your endurance you will gain your lives" (Luke 21:18–19). There may remain an instinctual fear of dying, of the dissolution of our body which was originally intended to be immortal. In reality, however, the end of our mortal life is only to be abhorred if we have rejected God definitively, for only from the second death will there be no resurrection (cf. Revelation 20:5–6; 12–15).

Redemption from sin having already been discussed in Chapter VI, it suffices to say here that all the acts of deliverance in the Old Testament, and particularly the exodus of the Israelites from Egypt, foreshadowed Christ's salvific work. The crossing of the Red Sea, which then drowned the enemies, points forward to the cleansing water of Baptism in which sin is destroyed. The power to forgive sins was the gift of the risen Lord to his apostles, to the Church for all time.

Evil has been overcome, as Pope Benedict explains:

> In Jesus' Passion, all the filth of the world touches the infinitely pure one, the soul of Jesus Christ and, hence, the Son of God himself ... Through this contact, the filth of the world is truly absorbed, wiped out, and transformed in the pain of infinite love. Because infinite good is now at hand in the man Jesus, the counterweight to all wickedness is present and active within world history, and the

good is always infinitely greater than the vast mass
of evil, however terrible it may be.[4]

Let us not forget that the holy sacrifice of the Mass makes
this counterweight to evil present, here and now.

In God's mysterious providence, however, there
remains a battle to be fought by every generation and each
individual. The war between good and evil will continue
on earth as long as time lasts. The Catechism speaks of
the Church's ultimate trial:

> Before Christ's second coming the church must
> pass through a final trial that will shake the faith of
> many believers. The persecution that accompanies
> her pilgrimage on earth will unveil the "mystery of
> iniquity", in the form of a religious deception
> offering men an apparent solution to their
> problems at the price of apostasy from the truth.[5]

Messianic hope can only be fully realized at the end of
time when Christ returns in glory:

> The kingdom will be fulfilled, then, not by a
> historic triumph of the Church through a
> progressive ascendancy, but only by God's victory
> over the final unleashing of evil, which will cause
> his Bride to come down from heaven. God's
> triumph over the revolt of evil will take the form
> of the Last Judgement after the final cosmic
> upheaval of this passing world.[6]

Until then, we continue to work and pray for deliverance
from evil. Cardinal Sarah has this contemplative insight:

---

4. Pope Benedict, *Jesus of Nazareth Part Two*, p. 231.

5. *CCC* 675.

6. *Ibid.*, 677.

The combat against evil plays out over time and it
is important to persevere and not to lose hope. God
is fashioning hearts, and evil never has the last
word. In the darkness God works in silence ... Let
us never forget that silent prayer is the strongest
and surest act in the struggle against evil.[7]

In addition to the saints interceding for us in heaven, we
have the good angels on our side. There is a prayer used
at the Office of Compline which we can make our own:
"Visit this house, we pray you, Lord, and drive far from it
all the snares of the enemy; may your holy angels dwell
here and guard us in peace, and may your blessing be
always upon us." Pope Francis has also encouraged us to
pray daily to St. Michael:

Holy Michael the archangel, defend us in the day
of battle, be our safeguard against the wickedness
and snares of the devil. May God rebuke him, we
humbly pray; and do thou, prince of the heavenly
host, by the power of God, thrust down to hell
Satan and all wicked spirits, who wander through
the world for the ruin of souls.

We each have a Guardian Angel ever at our side to protect
and guide us; devotion and attention to them will spare us
many a trouble. St Bernard assures us:

Though we are children and the road that lies
ahead of us is so long, and not only long but
dangerous, what have we to fear with such guard-
ians? They cannot be vanquished, nor led astray,
still less can they lead us astray, these beings who
guard us in all our ways. They are faithful, they are
wise, they are powerful; what have we to fear? Let

---

7.   Sarah, *The Power of Silence*, p. 152.

us but follow them and cling to them, and we shall abide in the shadow of the Almighty.[8]

There is significant, if at times subtle, evil in false ideologies. They are a form of rebellion against God, against the natural law, against truth. Our Lord described Satan as "a murderer from the beginning ... a liar and the father of lies" (John 8:44). In particular, the failure to recognise and protect human life in the womb, so prevalent throughout the world, bears the characteristic features of the Evil One: murder and falsehood. Christ entrusted to the Church the mission to teach the truth, a mission guided by the Holy Spirit, the Spirit of truth:

> so that we may no longer be children, tossed to and fro and carried about with every wind of doctrine, by the cunning of men, by their craftiness in deceitful wiles. Rather, speaking the truth in love, we are to grow up in every way into him who is the head, into Christ (Ephesians 4:14-15).

God is truth. It is noteworthy that liars are specified among those who are excluded from the heavenly Jerusalem. Truth is a vital force for good even if, following in the steps of the Master, it can lead to punishment and death in this world. Every conscientious act of honesty, every courageous defence of the truth, every humble confession of sin contributes to the defeat of evil. Similarly, praise and thanksgiving to God in all circumstances, together with trust in his loving providence, are weapons of righteousness. In the words of Jesus to St Faustina, "When a soul extols My goodness, Satan trembles before it and flees to the very bottom of hell."[9]

---

8. St Bernard, *Sermon 12 on Qui habitat [Psalm 91(90)]*, 9.

9. St Maria Faustina Kowalska, *Diary* (Stockbridge, MA: Marian Press, 2013), p. 172.

By praying and living the Lord's Prayer—having confidence in God our Father, praising his name in word and deed, praying and working for the coming of his kingdom, doing his will, feeding on the Eucharist, seeking and granting forgiveness and combating temptation—we will assuredly be delivered from evil. We will not be spared all adversity, sorrow, misfortune and illness, but God tells us, "in quietness and in trust shall be your strength" (Isaiah 30:15). If borne patiently, these trials will effect that purification of our soul which must otherwise be undergone in Purgatory after our death, for nothing unclean would be able to endure the unveiled vision of the all-holy God. Sufferings accepted will also contribute to both an eternal weight of glory beyond comparison with temporal afflictions (cf. 2 Corinthians 4:17), and the salvation of other souls.

Trusting in our Father then—and trust is the key to his heart—we can say confidently with St Paul, "The Lord will rescue me from every evil and save me for his heavenly kingdom" (2 Timothy 4:18). We have his divine assurance:

Fear not, for I have redeemed you;
    I have called you by name, you are mine.
When you pass through the waters I will be with you;
    and through the rivers, they shall not overwhelm you;
When you walk through fire you shall not be burned
    and the flame shall not consume you.
For I am the Lord your God,
    the Holy One of Israel, your Saviour (Isaiah 43:1–3).

Subheadings of the Biblical meditation which follows

- God's great act of deliverance from Egypt.
- Trust and confidence in God's saving power.
- Prayers for deliverance.
- God's wisdom gives protection against evil.
- Jesus' authority over demonic forces is given also to the apostles.
- Jesus is sovereign over death.
- Christ's victory over the devil gives peace and assurance to his followers.
- Our Lord's prayer to the Father for his disciples.
- Confidence in the victory of Christ in the midst of tribulation.
- Spiritual warfare against evil.
- The angels guard us.
- The role of the Archangel Michael in defeating Satan.
- Parable of the Last Judgment.
- Other images of the final and definitive defeat of evil and punishment of evildoers.
- The culmination of Christ's victory.

God's great act of deliverance from Egypt

Psalm 136(135):1, 10–11

> O give thanks to the Lord for he is good,
>> for his steadfast love endures for ever ...
> to him who smote the first-born of Egypt,
>> for his steadfast love endures for ever;
> and brought Israel out from among them,
>> for his steadfast love endures for ever.

Psalm 106(105):9–10

> He rebuked the Red Sea, and it became dry;
>> and he led them through the deep as through a desert.
> So he saved them from the hand of the foe,
>> and delivered them from the power of the enemy.

Trust and confidence in God's saving power

Psalm 97(96):10

> The Lord loves those who hate evil;
>> he preserves the lives of his saints;
>> he delivers them from the hand of the wicked.

1 Samuel 17:37

David said, "The Lord who delivered me from the paw of the lion and from the paw of the bear, will deliver me from the hand of this Philistine."

Daniel 3:17

Our God whom we serve is able to deliver us from the from the burning fiery furnace; and he will deliver us out of your hand, O king.

Prayers for deliverance

Esther 14:3

O my Lord, thou only art our King; help me, who am alone, and have no helper but thee, for my danger is in my hand.

Psalm 44(43):23–26

> Rouse thyself! Why sleepest thou, O Lord?
>> Awake! Do not cast us off for ever!
> Why dost thou hide they face?
>> Why dost thou forget our affliction and op-
>> pression?
> For our soul is bowed down to the dust,
>> our body cleaves to the ground.
> Rise up, come to our help!
>> Deliver us for the sake of thy steadfast love!

Psalm 71(70):1–4

> In thee, O Lord, do I take refuge;
>> let me never be put to shame!
> In thy righteousness deliver me and rescue me;
>> incline they ear to me, and save me!
> Be thou to me a rock of refuge,
>> a strong fortress to save me,
>> for thou art my rock and my fortress.
> Rescue me, O my God, from the hand of the wicked,
>> from the grasp of the unjust and cruel man.

God's wisdom gives protection against evil

Proverbs 2:6–15

> For the Lord gives wisdom;
>> from his mouth come knowledge and understanding;
> he stores up sound wisdom for the upright;

he is a shield to those who walk in integrity,
guarding the paths of justice
  and preserving the way of his saints.
Then you will understand righteousness and justice
  and equity, every good path;
for wisdom will come into your heart,
  and knowledge will be pleasant to your soul;
discretion will watch over you;
  and understanding will guard you;
delivering you from the way of evil,
    from men of perverted speech,
who forsake the paths of uprightness
    to walk in the ways of darkness,
who rejoice in doing evil
  and delight in the perverseness of evil;
men whose paths are crooked,
    and who are devious in their ways.

Jesus' authority over demonic forces is given also to the apostles

Acts 10:36–38

You know ... how God anointed Jesus of Nazareth with the Holy Spirit and with power; how he went about doing good and healing all who were oppressed by the devil, for God was with him.

Matthew 10:1

He called to him his twelve disciples and gave them authority over unclean spirits, to cast them out, and to heal every disease and every infirmity.

Jesus is sovereign over death

John 11:25–26

Jesus said to her, "I am the resurrection and the life; he who believes in me, though he die, yet shall he live, and whoever lives and believes in me shall never die."

Revelation 1:17–18

Fear not, I am the first and the last, and the living one; I died and behold I am alive for evermore, and I have the keys of Death and Hades.

Christ's victory over the devil gives peace and assurance to his followers

John 12:31

Now is the judgment of this world, now shall the ruler of this world be cast out.

John 14:27

Peace I leave with you; my peace I give to you; not as the world gives do I give to you. Let not your hearts be troubled, neither let them be afraid.

John 16:33

In the world you have tribulation; but be of good cheer, I have overcome the world.

Our Lord's prayer to the Father for his disciples

John 17:15

I do not pray that thou shouldst take them out of the world, but that thou shouldst keep them from the evil one.

Confidence in the victory of Christ in the midst of tribulation

Romans 8:31, 35–39

If God is for us, who is against us? ... Who shall separate us from the love of Christ? Shall tribulation, or distress, or persecution or famine, or nakedness, or peril, or sword? As it is written, "For thy sake we are being killed all the day long; we are regarded as sheep to be slaughtered." No, in all these things we are more than conquerors through him who loved us. For I am sure that neither death, nor life, nor angels, nor principalities, nor things present, nor things to come, nor power, nor height, nor depth, nor anything else in all creation, will be able to separate us from the love of God in Christ Jesus our Lord.

Spiritual warfare against evil

Ephesians 6:10–18

Be strong in the Lord and in the strength of his might. Put on the whole armour of God, that you may be able to stand against the wiles of the devil. For we are not contending against flesh and blood, but against the principalities, against the powers, against the world rulers of this present darkness, against the spiritual hosts of wickedness in the heavenly places. Therefore, take the whole armour of God, that you may be able to withstand in the evil day, and having done all, to stand. Stand, therefore, having girded your loins with truth, and having put on the breastplate of righteousness, and having shod your feet with the equipment of the gospel of peace; above all taking the shield of faith with which you can quench all the flaming darts of the evil one. And take the helmet of salvation, and the sword of the Spirit, which is the word of God. Pray at all times in the Spirit, with all prayer and supplication. To that end keep alert with all perseverance.

The angels guard us

Exodus 23:20, 22

Behold I send an angel before you, to guard you on the way and to bring you to the place which I have prepared … if you hearken attentively to his voice and do all I say, then I will be an enemy to your enemies and an adversary to your adversaries.

Psalm91(90):9–13

> Because you have made the Lord your refuge,
>   the Most High your habitation,
> no evil shall befall you,
>   no scourge come near your tent.
> For he will give his angels charge of you
>   to guard you in all your ways.
> On their hands they will bear you up,
>   lest you dash your foot against a stone.
> You will tread on the lion and the adder,
>   the young lion and the serpent you will trample
>   underfoot.

Acts 12:11

Peter came to himself and said, "Now I am sure that the Lord has sent his angel and rescued me from the hand of Herod and all that the Jewish people were expecting."

The role of the Archangel Michael in defeating Satan

Revelation 12:7–9

Now war arose in heaven, Michael and his angels fighting against the dragon; and the dragon and his angels fought, but they were defeated and there was no longer any place for them in heaven. And the great dragon was thrown down, that ancient serpent, who is called the Devil and Satan, the deceiver of the whole world—he was thrown down to the earth and his angels were thrown down with him.

Daniel 12:1

At that time shall arise Michael, the great prince who has charge of your people. And there shall be a time of trouble, such as never has been seen since there was a nation till that time; but at that time your people shall be delivered, every one whose name shall be found written in the book.

Parable of the Last Judgment

Matthew 13: 36–43

"Explain to us the parable of the weeds of the field." He answered, "Hewho sows the good seed is the Son of man; the field is the world, and the good seed means the sons of the kingdom; the weeds are the sons of the evil one, and the enemy who sowed them is the devil; the harvest is the close of the age, and the reapers are the angels. Just as the weeds are gathered and burned with fire, so will it be at the close of the age. The Son of man will send his angels, and they will gather out of his kingdom all causes of sin and all evildoers, and throw them into the furnace of fire; there men will weep and gnash their teeth. Then the righteous will shine like the sun in the kingdom of their Father. He who has ears, let him hear."

Other images of the final and definitive defeat of evil and punishment of evildoers

Revelation 17:13–14

These are of one mind and give over their power and authority to the beast; they will make war on the Lamb, and the Lamb will conquer them, for he is the Lord of lords and King of kings, and those with him are called and chosen and faithful.

Revelation 20:9–10

They marched up over the broad earth and surrounded the camp of the saints and the beloved city; but fire came down from heaven and consumed them, and the devil who had deceived them was thrown into the lake of fire and brimstone where the beast and false prophet were, and they will be tormented day and night for ever and ever.

Revelation 21:8

As for the cowardly, the faithless, the polluted, as for murderers, fornicators, sorcerers, idolaters, and all liars, their lot shall be in the lake that burns with fire and brimstone, which is the second death.

The culmination of Christ's victory

1 Corinthians 15:24–25

Then comes the end, when he delivers the kingdom to God the Father after destroying every rule and every authority and power. For he must reign until he has put all his enemies under his feet.

IX

Amen

Through our Lord Jesus Christ, your Son,
who lives and reigns with you in the unity of the
Holy Spirit,
one God for ever and ever.

Conclusion to Collects

I n concluding the prayer with the Hebrew word *amen*,
which means "so be it", we confirm our commitment
to all the petitions we have expressed. Amen is a title
Our Lord gives himself: "The words of the Amen, the
faithful and true witness, the beginning of God's creation"
(Revelation 3:14). Our promise of faithfulness is, therefore,
a response to his unshakeable trustworthiness and
dependent upon it. "He is the definitive 'Amen' of the
Father's love for us. He takes up and completes our 'Amen'
to the Father."[1] In the words of St Paul:

> For the Son of God, Jesus Christ, whom we
> preached among you ... was not Yes and No; but
> in him it was always Yes. For all the promises of
> God find their Yes in him. That is why we utter the
> Amen through him to the glory of God (2 Corin-
> thians 1:19–20).

---

1.   *CCC* 1065

Therefore we pray, "Lord, do thou say Amen! Bring the Amen to life within me — as truth, deeply rooted; fidelity which does not waver; resolution which does not tire!"[2]

2.   Romano Guardini, *The Lord's Prayer* (London: Burns & Oates, 1958), p. 125.

The Blessed Virgin Mary in Relation to the Our Father

O God, who made the Mother of your Son
to be our Mother and Queen,
graciously grant that, sustained by her inter-
cession,
we may attain in the heavenly Kingdom
the glory promised to your children.

Collect, 22nd August

Praying the Our Father in the light of sacred Scripture, we cannot overlook the discreet presence of Our Lady. The one who was wholly at God's disposal, who sang his praise in her canticle, who contemplated the mysteries of her Son in her heart, who interceded for human needs at Cana, who offered her sufferings at the foot of the cross in union with the Redeemer, who prayed with the apostles and other holy women for the coming of the Holy Spirit at Pentecost, she leads us along the way of prayer.

Our Father who art in heaven

As we saw earlier, the prophet Isaiah likens the tenderness of God to that of a woman, a mother, and one of the Hebrew words used in the Old Testament for God's mercy is derived from the word for a mother's womb.[1] It can be said that Mary is the most direct representative of this feminine aspect of the Father. Moreover, we can see an interplay between Mary as Mother and as daughter, highlighted in her privileged relationship with the Blessed Trinity. "She is endowed with the high office and dignity of being the Mother of the Son of God and therefore she is also the beloved daughter of the Father and temple of the Holy Spirit."[2] Pope St John Paul II comments on this text, "Mary is the 'beloved daughter of the Father' in a unique way. She has been granted an utterly special likeness between her motherhood and the divine fatherhood"[3]; for the Son of God is also the Son of Mary.

Furthermore, it is through Mary's motherhood of Christ in the Incarnation that we have become adopted children of God and can invoke God as our Father:

> When the time had fully come, God sent forth his Son, born of woman, born under the law, to redeem those who were under the law, so that we might receive adoption as sons. And because you are sons, God has sent the Spirit of his Son into our hearts, crying, 'Abba! Father!' (Galatians 4:4–6).

In addition, she has become our mother too, for on the Cross, Jesus gave her to be the mother of all his disciples in the person of St John: "'Woman, behold, your son!' Then he said to the disciple, 'Behold, your mother!'" (John 19:26–27).

The greeting of the Angel Gabriel at the Annunciation has profound implications, for it suggests that Mary is also the personification of the "Daughter of Zion" spoken of by

1. Cf. Pope St John Paul II, *Dives in Misericordia*, note 52.
2. Vatican II, *Lumen Gentium*, 53.
3. Pope St John Paul II, *General Audience* (10 January 1996).

the prophets. The word usually translated as "Hail" in Luke 1:28 is more accurately rendered "Rejoice". In her, the messianic prophecies are fulfilled: "Sing aloud, O daughter of Zion; shout O Israel! Rejoice and exult with all your heart, O daughter of Jerusalem! ... The King of Israel, the Lord is in your midst; you shall fear evil no more" (Zephaniah 3:14–15; see also Zechariah 2:10, 9:9). Mary is the representative both of Israel her people and of mankind as a whole as she receives the salutation.

Hallowed be thy name

In Mary's *Magnificat*, we see intertwined the praise of God's name and her own blessedness:

> My soul glorifies the Lord, and my spirit rejoices in God my Saviour, for he has regarded the low estate of his handmaiden. For behold, henceforth all generations will call me blessed; for he who is mighty has done great things for me, and holy is his name (Luke 1:46–49).

She, "full of grace" and without sin, is the one who can most perfectly praise and glorify God, with her lips and with her life. On the other hand, as Cardinal Ratzinger points out:

> The Church neglects one of the duties enjoined upon her when she does not praise Mary. She deviates from the words of the Bible when her Marian devotion falls silent. When this happens, in fact, the Church no longer even glorifies God as she ought ... Mary is one of the human beings who in an altogether special way belongs to the name

of God, so much so, in fact, that we cannot praise him rightly if we leave her out of account.[4]

Thy kingdom come

The Blessed Virgin was the recipient of the announcement that the Messiah was to be born of her, that her Son was to be King: "The Lord God will give to him the throne of his father David, and he will reign over the house of Jacob for ever; and of his kingdom, there will be no end" (Luke 1:32–33). It was her divine motherhood which made possible the inauguration of God's reign in person. She is best fitted to mother the growth of God's kingdom in our hearts and in our world.

In the *Magnificat*, we have a portrayal of fundamental aspects of this kingdom, described thus by St John Henry Newman:

> Take St Mary's hymn, which we read every evening; she was no woman of high estate, the nursling of palaces and the pride of a people, yet she was chosen to an illustrious place in the Kingdom of heaven. So she spoke of His "scattering the proud," "putting down the mighty," "exalting the humble and meek," "filling the hungry with good things," and "sending the rich empty away." This was a shadow or outline of that Kingdom of the Spirit, which was then coming on the earth.[5]

The humble handmaid of the Lord was one of the blessed "poor in spirit" to whom the kingdom belongs. Yet she is also Queen. "Thy throne, O God, is for ever and ever; the sceptre of thy kingdom is a sceptre of uprightness ... The

---

4. Ratzinger, *Mary – The Church at the source*, pp. 62–63.

5. St John Henry Newman, *PS.*, VI, 22, "The Weapons of Saints," p. 314.

queen stood on thy right hand, in gilded clothing" (Psalm 44:7,9).[6] In the book of Revelation, we are given a vision of a woman in heaven, "clothed with the sun, with the moon under her feet, and on her head a crown of twelve stars" (12:1). While this has multiple layers of interpretation, the Church understands one of them to be a portrayal of Our Lady in glory: "See the queen wearing the crown with which her Son has crowned her."[7] It is reminiscent of a line from the Song of Songs which is used in the monastic Office for the feast of the Assumption: "Who is she that cometh forth as the morning rising, fair as the moon, bright as the sun?" (6:9).[8]

Thy will be done on earth as it is in heaven

"Behold, I am the handmaid of the Lord; let it be to me according to your word" (Luke 1:38). At the Annunciation, Mary anticipated and made her own, the readiness of her Son to obey the will and word of God. She became the New Eve, repairing the disobedience of the first Eve. Christ made the fulfilment of the Father's will and word a form of kinship with himself: "Whoever does the will of my Father in heaven is my brother, and sister, and mother" (Matthew 12:50); and, "My mother and my brethren are those who hear the word of God and do it" (Luke 8:21). Mary was his Mother according to both the flesh and the spirit in her perfect obedience, maintained all the way to the foot of the Cross, in union with her Son's.

---

6. Douay Rheims Bible.
7. St Bernard, *Sermon for the Sunday within the Octave of the Assumption*, 7.
8. Douay Rheims Bible.

"Blessed is she who believed that there would be a fulfilment of what was spoken to her from the Lord" (Luke 1:45). Cardinal Ratzinger extols her faith:

> Mary is the great believer who humbly offered herself to God as an empty vessel for him to use in his mysterious plan. Without complaint she surrendered control of her life; she did not try to live according to human calculation but put herself completely at the disposal of God's mysterious, incomprehensible design. All she wanted to be was the handmaid of the Lord, the instrument and servant of the Word. Therein lies her true fame: that she remained a believer despite all the darkness and all the inexplicable demands God made on her.[9]

Give us this day our daily bread

"Ask and it will be given you" (Luke 11:9). The intervention of the Mother of Jesus at the wedding feast at Cana shows the concern she had for those in need and the fruitfulness of her mediation. In heaven she continues her work of maternal charity.

It has been suggested, however, that at Cana she was asking not only for material wine, but for the wine of salvation.[10] Isaiah speaks of the earth laid waste by the Lord, and desolate: "There is an outcry in the streets for lack of wine; all joy has reached its eventide; the gladness of the earth is banished" (24:11). In contrast, a banquet of salvation is promised: "On this mountain, the Lord of hosts will make for all peoples a feast of fat things, a feast of wine on the lees, of fat things full of marrow, of wine on the lees well refined" (25:6), and it is associated with the de-

---

9.   Ratzinger, *Dogma and Preaching*, p. 110.

10.   Pitre, *Jesus the Bridegroom*, pp. 39–43.

struction of death and sorrow (v. 8). Hence Our Lord's reply, "My hour has not yet come" (John 2:4) — the hour of his Passion, when the wine of salvation, his blood, would be given definitively. The miracle at Cana, worked at his Mother's request, anticipated this hour and pointed forward to it. Thus we can entrust our spiritual as well as our bodily needs to the tender care of this powerful advocate.

"He has filled the hungry with good things" (Luke 1:53). Pope St John Paul referred to Our Lady as "Woman of the Eucharist." She was "the first 'tabernacle' in history as she bore the Word made flesh in her womb".[11] It was she who gave her Son the human body and blood which we receive in Holy Communion. Commenting on the words of the *Ave Verum*, "Hail, true body born of the Virgin Mary," on the feast of Corpus Christi, he said, "If the Body that we eat and the Blood that we drink is the inestimable gift of the risen Lord to us travellers, it still has in itself, as fragrant Bread, the taste and aroma of the Virgin Mother."[12]

Forgive us our trespasses
as we forgive those who trespass against us

Mary stands out as the one who has received the mercy of God in the most perfect way. "Full of grace", conceived immaculate without original sin and sinless throughout her life, she was nevertheless redeemed by Christ, by virtue of his foreseen merits.

> She is the first in the order of mercy received, the first of the redeemed, the first of the forgiven. She is the Mother of all those souls who receive mercy

---

11.   Pope St John Paul II, *Ecclesia de Eucharistia*, 53, 55.
12.   Pope St John Paul II, *Angelus Address* (5 June 1983).

... She is, and remains, the Mother of Mercy
Incarnate in her Son Jesus.[13]

She is, therefore, not distant from us, poor sinners, but
close, ever interceding for our repentance, forgiveness and
conversion of heart.

As the one who stood by the Cross, watching her Son
die a tortuous death, pierced by the sword of sorrow to the
depths of her heart and soul, she knows more deeply than
any other human person the cost of forgiving the sins of
others. She consented to the offering Jesus made of his life
for the redemption of the world. She suffered in her spirit
the death he suffered in his body. May she lead us along
the path of forgiveness which leads to peace in this world
and eternal life in heaven.

And lead us not into temptation

"Watch and pray that you may not enter into temptation"
(Matthew 26:41). "I have laid up thy word in my heart, that
I might not sin against thee" (Psalm 119 (118):11). As we
have seen, these two texts give us the key to resistance in
temptation: vigilant prayer and meditation on the word of
God. The Mother of God both shows us the way by her
example and aids us with her intercession. St John Henry
Newman writes of her advocacy before God, "This is why
the Blessed Virgin is called 'Powerful' — nay sometimes, 'All-
Powerful', because she has, more than anyone else, more than
all Angels and Saints, this great, prevailing gift of prayer."[14]

---

13. Dom Xavier Perrin OSB, *The Radiance of her Face* (Kettering,
    OH: Angelico Press 2017), pp. 55–56.
14. St John Henry Newman, *Meditations and Devotions,* On the
    Assumption, 5 (London: Longmans, Green and Co. Ltd, 1960),
    p. 71.

Among the readings in the Church's lectionary for Masses of Our Lady is one from Sirach, which concludes, "Whoever obeys me will not be put to shame, and those who work with my help will not sin" (24:22). The advice she gives to us is that given to the servants at Cana, "Do whatever he tells you" (John 2:5).

But deliver us from evil

The fact that, in St John's Gospel, at Cana and Calvary, Our Lord calls his Mother "Woman" is significant.[15] This title links her with the woman of Genesis (Chapter 3), the woman of Revelation (Chapter 12), and with all the great women of the Old Testament; we can think particularly of Judith and Queen Esther who won decisive victories for the salvation of their people. The words of praise addressed to Judith are applied to the Blessed Virgin Mary in the liturgy:

> O daughter, you are blessed by the Most High above all women on earth; and blessed be the Lord God, who created the heavens and the earth, who has guided you to strike the head of the leader of our enemies. Your hope[16] will never depart from the hearts of men, as they remember the power of God (Judith 13:18–19).

In Genesis, immediately after the Fall, God gives a prophecy, a promise of redemption, addressing the serpent thus, "I will put enmity between you and the woman, and between your seed and her seed, he shall

---

15. It is noteworthy also that in this Gospel, she is never called by her name, but "the Mother of Jesus", as if to denote that her personal identity has been completely absorbed into her role as the Mother of the God who saves.

16. Our Latin text has "praise" (*laus*) here, rather than "hope".

bruise your head, and you shall bruise his heel" (3:15). In the Vulgate and other old Latin manuscripts, the reading, "he shall bruise" is rendered, "she shall bruise". This was taken as a direct reference to Our Lady, hence the pictures and statues of her standing on the head of the serpent. "He shall bruise" refers to Christ, but as his Mother, Mary's role is still vital. Moreover, through her Immaculate Conception and life-long sinlessness, she is unique in being the only human person wholly and always opposed to Satan. He never had the slightest hold on her and therefore she is his implacable adversary. St John of the Cross asserts that, "The devil fears a soul united to God as he does God Himself."[17] No one has ever been, or ever will be, more closely united to God than his Mother. Exorcists confirm her powerful influence in the battle against the author of all evil.

St John Henry Newman again emphasises the role of her prayer in this context:

> Her office is one of perpetual intercession for the faithful militant, and ... in the eternal enmity which exists between the woman and the serpent, while the serpent's strength lies in being the Tempter, the weapon of the Second Eve and Mother of God is prayer.[18]

There is an ancient prayer, dating from the third century and still in current use, which invokes her aid: "We fly to thy patronage, O holy Mother of God; despise not our prayers in our necessities, but deliver us from all dangers, O glorious and ever blessed Virgin."

---

17. St John of the Cross, Maxims on Love, 47, *The Collected Works of St John of the Cross* (Washington, D.C: ICS Publications, 1973), p. 677.

18. St John Henry Newman, *Difficulties of Anglicans* (London: Basil Montagu Pickering, 1876), p. 73.

It is the Rosary, however, drawn largely from Biblical texts including the Our Father, and at once Marian, Christological and Trinitarian, which is most strongly and frequently recommended, both by popes and by the Blessed Virgin herself. It has proved its worth over the centuries as a miraculous channel of heavenly assistance in the face of every danger and distress. In the conclusion to his Apostolic Letter on the Most Holy Rosary, Pope St John Paul quotes the "Supplication to the Queen of the Holy Rosary" by Bl. Bartolo Longo: "O Blessed Rosary of Mary, sweet chain which unites us to God, bond of love which unites us to the angels, tower of salvation against the assaults of Hell, safe port in our universal shipwreck, we will never abandon you."[19] And our heavenly Mother, Health of the sick, Refuge of sinners, Comfort of the afflicted, Help of Christians and Cause of our joy, will never abandon us.

No one has extolled her unfailing aid more eloquently than St Bernard:

> In dangers, in hardships, in every doubt, think of Mary, call out to Mary. Keep her in your mouth, keep her in your heart. Follow the example of her life, and you will obtain the favour of her prayer. Following her, you will never go astray. Asking her help, you will never despair. Keeping her in your thoughts, you will never wander away. With your hand in hers, you will never stumble. With her protecting you, you will not be afraid. With her leading you, you will never tire. Her kindness will see you through to the end.[20]

---

19. Pope St John Paul *Rosarium Virginis Mariæ*, 43.

20. St Bernard, *Homilies in Praise of the Virgin Mother* II, 17, in *Magnificat* (Michigan: Cistercian Publications Inc., 1979), pp. 30–31.

Amen

We pray this in union with Our Lady, Mother of Christ and Mother of the Church.

> Mary's "Fiat" is the source of our "Fiat". It is the joy of heaven and the three persons of the Blessed Trinity; it is the joy of Christ, of his Church and of us all.
>
> May our "Amen" bring joy to our Mother ... May it through her bring joy to God himself.[21]

---

21. Stefan Cardinal Wyszynski, "*Our Father ...*" (Slough: St Paul Publications, 1982), p. 109.